Thracian Tales

GEORGIOS VIZYENOS

Thracian Tales

Translated by
Peter Mackridge

AIORA

Peter Mackridge is Emeritus Professor of Modern Greek at the University of Oxford. He has published several books on modern Greek language and literature, including two co-authored grammars. His translations of stories by the 19th-century author Alexandros Papadiamandis and a collection of haikus by the 21st-century poet Haris Vlavianos are due to be published in 2014.

Drawing on page 15 by Eleonora Spathopoulou.

Original titles of the short stories:

> Το μόνον της ζωής του ταξίδιον
> Το αμάρτημα της μητρός μου
> Ποίος ήτον ο φονεύς του αδελφού μου

© Aiora Press 2014

ISBN : 978-618-5048-16-7

AIORA PRESS
11 Mavromichali st.
Athens 10679 - Greece
tel: +30 210 3839000
www.aiora.gr

Contents

Introduction

Thrace is a corner of south-east Europe where Greece, Bulgaria and Turkey meet. The Greek writer Georgios (George) Vizyenos was born there in 1849. As a child he was simply called "Mick's son, Georgie", but as an adult he adopted the surname by which he became known as a writer. "Vizyenos" means "the man from Vizye", after the small town in Thrace where he was born and spent his early years. Vizye (Vize in Turkish) is situated between Constantinople (Istanbul), about 85 miles to the south-east, and Adrianople (Edirne), which today is near the border with Bulgaria. Vizye was then, and still is today, in Turkey, but in those days it had a sizeable Greek population, as did Constantinople, which was the capital of the Ottoman empire.

Vizyenos had a curious life and career. His father, a pedlar, died when George was five years old; two of his sisters perished in early childhood; and one of his brothers died in mysterious circumstances. So as not to be a burden to his widowed mother, and so as to supplement the family's meagre income, George left home at the age of ten to be apprenticed to a tailor in Istanbul. After following this trade for eight years he was singled out by a succession of

rich Greek patrons who were struck by his exceptional in-
tellectual talents and decided to encourage them. He began
studying for the priesthood, but he abandoned this voca-
tion and at the age of twenty-four he entered high school
in Athens and in the same year published his first book of
poetry and completed his second.

After spending a year at school, he entered Athens University, but he became dissatisfied with his studies there and
in 1875 he went to Germany, where he completed his education at the universities of Göttingen, Leipzig and Berlin
– still supported by rich patrons – with a dissertation on
the psychology of children's play. After a further period of
study in London and Paris, Vizyenos returned to Greece
with the aim of becoming a university lecturer in the his-
tory of philosophy. However, he failed to fulfil this ambition
and instead taught in high schools until 1890, when he was
appointed Professor of Drama at the Athens Conservatoire.

By this time Vizyenos had established himself as a poet
and fiction-writer, but he was made to feel an outsider in
the literary and academic world of Athens. The tragedies
and privations of his early life, his extraordinary rise from
tailor's assistant to doctor of philosophy, and the professional and personal difficulties he encountered on the way
led to grave mental instability, and, one day in 1892, having
conceived a passion for a teenage girl, he was found dressed
as a bridegroom and claiming that he was about to marry
her. He spent the last four years of his life in Daphni mental
asylum, where he died in 1896.

Vizyenos' prose work consists of six long stories, of
which the first five (including the three included in this volume) appeared in the Athens magazine *Estia* in 1883 and

1884. His first story, "My mother's sin", was one of the earliest examples of the genre to be published in Greece.

The three stories published in this volume are all set in Thrace, and they are all narrated by Yorgis, whose name is a familiar form of the author's own Christian name. The three stories concern members of Yorgis' family and thus their themes are interconnected. "The one and only journey of his life" centres round Yorgis' eccentric maternal grandfather; "Who was my brother's murderer?" concerns especially Yorgis' brother Christakis; and the boys' mother is the chief character in "My mother's sin". The extent to which Vizyenos' stories are autobiographical is beside the point, but, as he became acquainted with novels and stories in English, French and German, he no doubt came to realize that the experiences his family had undergone were the stuff of fiction. His decision to specialize in the study of psychology must have been influenced by his desire to explore the influences that his family tragedies had had on his own psyche, and his account of the narrator's relationship with his pathologically obsessive mother in two of his stories probably draws on a combination of his own childhood memories and his academic study of the effects of traumatic experiences.

Something that strikes the reader on *re*-reading Vizyenos is the care with which he dispenses information. At the basis of his writing is a realization that much of human action is enigmatic and possibly inexplicable, and that an attempt to discover the motivations of people's actions can often lead to harrowing psychological consequences for the person carrying out the investigation. All of Vizyenos' stories are tales of the unexpected, and at the end of each

one the narrator finds himself in possession of some
knowledge that forces him – and the reader – to revise
their earlier assumptions, which had been based on in-
complete knowledge. Because Vizyenos wants us too to experience the difficult transition from ignorance to knowledge, he deliberately leaves us in a state of uncertainty until
the very end of the story.

In every case the transition from the narrator's state of
false illusion (usually as a child) to his consciousness of the
true situation (as an adult) is brought about by a long nar-
ration on the part of another character. At the time when
Vizyenos was writing, the use of *katharevousa* (an artificial
compromise between Ancient and Modern Greek) was *de
rigueur* in fiction. While Vizyenos doesn't deviate from this
norm in the main narrative, the dialogue and the characters'
narrations are presented in the spoken language. The gap
between these two varieties of Greek , which is difficult to
convey adequately in English, indicates the cultural gap that
separates the educated adult Yorgis (and, by extension,
Vizyenos himself) from the world in which he grew up.
(Indicative of this is the fact that in "Who was my brother's
murderer?" Yorgis' mother mocks his new-fangled surname
– which is, by implication, "Vizyenos" – for being "highfalutin".) I should add that the *katharevousa* of the main narrative is much easier to translate than the oral language used
by the characters. This is because, although *katharevousa*
was based on Greek words and forms, its ways of thinking
and modes of expression were modelled on western
European languages, particularly French and German. The
result is that the narrator's discourse is much closer to
English (albeit nineteenth-century English) than is the lan-

guage of the characters, which is colloquial, idiomatic, and more specifically Balkan in both feeling and expression.

The characters who narrate their stories to Yorgis see their "confession" as a cathartic and therapeutic act (a "talking cure", to use the term coined by "Anna O.", the patient of the pioneering Austrian psychoanalyst Josef Breuer in the early 1890s) that releases them from their burden of pent-up knowledge and emotion relating to some psychological trauma. At the end of each story, by putting the various characters' confessions together, Yorgis finds that he is the only person who possesses the solution to the initial mystery. The result of this, however, is that now he is burdened with some knowledge he wishes he didn't possess. For this reason he narrates *his* story, as a kind of writing therapy, so as to give it some coherence and to share it with us. In one of the stories in this volume – the only one in which comedy prevails despite a touch of pathos – the enigma posed in the title (what was the one and only journey of whose life?) is completely solved at the end; but in the other two Yorgis and the reader are finally left with a different conundrum, of a moral rather than a factual nature. What really constituted his mother's sin? Who was truly responsible for his brother's murder? These are the questions that Yorgis is unable to discuss with his mother, and in both cases the narrator concludes that they are ultimately unanswerable. The horrors depicted in "Who was my brother's murderer?" are worthy of Edgar Allan Poe, but the most horrific of all is the narrator's final realization of the truth.

A central theme of Vizyenos' stories is compassion. The mother who has sworn to take violent vengeance against her son's killer sublimates her passion through extraordinary acts of compassion. The narrator himself shows remarkable compassion for the Turk Kamil, whose sufferings in love outstrip even those of Vizyenos himself. It is tempting to see Kamil as a symbolic *alter ego* of the author, while Yorgis is his more realistic counterpart.

It is striking that in "Who was my brother's murderer?" Yorgis initially expresses a conventional Greek distaste for the Turks, but gradually, through personal contact with individual Turkish characters (namely Kamil and his mother), he comes to sympathize with their plight. His initial attitude, born of ignorance and prejudice, is radically modified by experience. The compassion with which Vizyenos depicts these Turkish characters, not as stereotypes but as suffering individuals, was one of my chief motivations in translating these stories.

The stories contained in this volume take place in and around Vizye and in Constantinople. "Who was my brother's murderer?" is set at a time when the Ottoman empire was struggling to survive. It contains references to the Russo-Turkish War of 1877-8, during which there was fighting around the recently opened Edirne-Istanbul railway, which passed a few miles from Vizye. In the same story there are also references to the Young Ottoman movement (not to be confused with the early-twentieth-century Young Turk movement), which aimed at ensuring the continuation of the empire by means of political reform and modernization.

Peter Mackridge
Oxford, December 2013

The one and only journey of his life

When they recruited me into the honourable profession of tailoring, none of their promises made a more attractive impression on my childish imagination than their assurance that at Constantinople I was to make dresses for the King's daughter.

I knew full well that princesses have a special weakness for apprentice tailors, especially when the latter know how to sing the praises of their charms as they stitch the fine silks with which the young ladies adorn their beauty.

I knew that when a princess falls in love with her tailor-boy it's no laughing matter: she falls head over heels in love; she becomes ill; she reaches death's door; and no doctor can cure her, no witch can restore her to health. And finally she calls her father and tells him bluntly, "Daddy, either I marry the little tailor who sings so beautifully, or I die!"

The King has no other children, so he has no alternative but to put his crown on his head and fall at the feet of the tailor-boy, crying, "For the love of God, I beseech you to take my daughter's hand. I beseech you to become my son-in-law. But first perform some heroic deed so I don't lose my reputation – after all, I *am* a king."

The young tailor feels as though he has an unripe medlar stuck in his throat and he can't swallow. The fact is, though, that there's nothing stuck in his throat, but he's so frightened to see the King wearing his crown that his saliva has dried up.

The King, wearing his crown, pats the young tailor on the shoulder, asks him what he is capable of doing, and waits with the utmost joy to hear that his prospective son-in-law can bring a lion down from the mountains alive, or kill a dragon, or conquer a kingdom.

Thereupon the young tailor takes courage, but is not so carried away as to contemplate being torn to pieces by wild beasts in order to become His Majesty's son-in-law. The young tailor is on the whole a peaceable fellow, and since he manages better when he sings than when he talks, he answers the King in song:

"Oh I can sew the wedding clothes
without a single stitch."

"Very well, you scoundrel!" thinks the King, who doesn't take too much to singing. "I'll teach you to turn my little girl's head when you haven't got an ounce of heroism in you!" Then he gives the apprentice a fierce look. "Very well, son-in-law!" he says, "make me forty suits of wedding clothes fit for a princess's wedding, and make sure I can't see a single stitch, a single thread anywhere. See you have them ready first thing tomorrow morning, before sunrise, otherwise I'll cut off your head!"

The King, wearing his crown, is taking things very seriously. The ambitious fellow is determined to kill the young tailor and give his daughter's hand to a great nobleman.

Luckily the young tailor has no doubt he will succeed,

so he isn't too worried. For he is – some say the son, some
the grandson of the Fairy Queen. And he has a thimble that
he never removes from his finger.

All that evening he eats, drinks and enjoys himself. In
the middle of the night, when the master tailor and his apprentices are asleep, he takes the thimble off his finger, pulls
out a golden hair that he keeps inside it, and burns the tip
in the lamp-flame. Immediately the golden-haired Fairy
Queen appears before him.

"What is it that distresses you, my dear?"

And the young tailor relates the story to her.

The golden-haired Fairy Queen, who has promised to
save him whenever he is in danger, claps her white hands
three times and, lo and behold! forty fairies dressed in
white, each one lovelier than the next, singing sweetly and
swaying coquettishly, place before the tailor-boy the most
precious cloths in the whole world.

The young tailor cuts the cloth and the fairies sew; and
as they sew they sing and joke and tease the lad so
amorously and temptingly that if their mother wasn't
nearby they would surely turn his head. But the golden-
haired Fairy Queen watches over them, instructs them and
urges them on, so that they finish the wedding clothes before the cock crows and the sun rises.

No sooner have the fairies left than in comes the King
with his crown on his head and the executioners at his
heels: he's come to slaughter the young tailor! But as soon
as he comes in he sees the forty wedding suits hanging on
the line without a single stitch and he can't believe his eyes,
for the gold and the pearls embroidered into them are
worth his whole paltry kingdom.

The King, wearing his crown, bites his lip. He takes the young tailor by the arm, leads him to the palace and hands over his daughter, and that's the end of the story.

All this was related to me by my grandfather. He used to tell the story as if it had happened but yesterday, and as if it was happening at every moment in the world. I still remember the childish pride with which I entered the city for the first time as a new recruit in the tailors' guild, thinking how in a few days' time I would be parading through the very gate through which I was now walking, triumphantly accompanying the most beautiful princess to my village. This last detail was also suggested to me by grandfather, and since grandfather was the most travelled and worldly-wise person I knew, I believed what he said to the last iota.

Nonetheless, many months passed since my arrival without anything being achieved. It is true that my master was chief tailor to the Queen Mother, the Validé Sultana, and since I was the youngest of his apprentices, he used to send me regularly to her palace on the Bosporus, sometimes carrying a large package on my head, sometimes holding under my arm the silk bag with gold tassels that contained his ledger. Thus I would often walk through luxurious arcades and, by way of shady passages, I would penetrate into the magical, perfumed apartment of the Validé Sultana's harem. But the creatures with whom I came in contact there were chiefly the black eunuchs, with their broad mouths, their huge teeth shining unnervingly white between their thick lips, and wild glances which made me tremble with horror. Sometimes "they" – the princesses, doubtless – wished to express particular gratitude towards their young tailor. Then the most fearsome of the blackamoors would grasp his whip, beckon me and lead the way. I would follow, my eyes riveted to the floor. A second blackamoor with a second whip would follow close behind. In this way, between these two executioners, I used to venture into the innermost areas of the harem, in which, however, I saw nothing but the floor, which was sometimes shining like that of the finest ball-room, sometimes covered with sumptuous carpets.

Though I saw nothing, I at least used to hear. I heard female voices, laughter, ribald comments and curses directed at the chief eunuch of the harem walking in front of me, who would shout at the top of his voice that the handmaidens and odalisques of the Sultana should hide themselves away at my approach, and who would lash out mercilessly with his whip at any who dared to peep through the doors and curtains to see a male creature coming so close to them. The Ethiopian who followed me protected me from being snatched away by those who stealthily and recklessly followed behind, while at the same time watching me in case I dared to raise my eyes from the ground and sully with my infidel glance the sacred victims who were destined to be sacrificed to some passing whim of their great Master.

Amid such excitements I would finally arrive at my destination. But there, in the last of the rooms, where the blackamoors left me, closing the door behind me, what do you think awaited me? Some rosy-cheeked blonde princess ready to jump for joy into my arms? There was nothing, absolutely nothing in the room; but in the wall separating the room from the next a wooden cylinder waited for me to caress it and pat it as if it were my mistress. This cylinder was constructed in such a way as to revolve on a vertical pivot without allowing one to see past it into the next room. As soon as I had caressed it, a soft voice would be heard from within:

"Have you come, my lamb?"

"Yes, Sultana."

The wooden cylinder would turn, presenting me on its opposite side with a small door that made it look like a cupboard. Patchouli, musk, amber and all the perfumes of the Indies floated fragrantly behind that door. Surely my princess must be there! I would anxiously open the door, whereupon inside this small cupboard there would be waiting a sweet-smelling, tasty *muhallebi*, a *börek*, a *baklava*, or another of those sweets which, though they cannot speak, seem as soon as you see them to be saying "Eat me". Which, of course, I did without more ado.

One day, as soon as this pleasant task was over, the soft voice asked me if I wanted something even better.

"No, Sultana, I want nothing better than you."

"Oh good, my lamb! Tell me, are you a big lad?"

I was about to tell her that I was just small enough to climb into the little cupboard, close the door, give a turn to the cylinder and appear like a *börek* before her eyes, when the black eunuch, who meanwhile had entered with my noticing, let out a curse over my head, stifling my voice in my throat.

My poor princess had to receive the answer from his fierce and awesome mouth:

"A big lad, eh? Ha, ha, ha," roared the eunuch with a sardonic laugh. "He's so small that to hang him high, at the level of my eyes, I've had to order a new stool for him to stand on."

Then he beckoned me to follow him.

Now if the Validé Sultana, like certain Asian kings of old, had a wise scribe at every door of her palace, with orders to record in the most florid terms everything that occurred around him, I doubt not but that each and every one of them would have noted in his chronicle that on that day I left the harem, as usual, with one eunuch in front, driving the odalisques away from my sight, the other following and fending off those who were trying to grasp on to my clothes from behind. I can assert, however, that as soon as the fearful negro said he had ordered a new stool to hang me, the floor of the room suddenly receded beneath my feet, and I was plunged into dark and silent chaos, with the giddiness and faintness that we feel when we dream we are falling, falling, falling from the immeasurable height of a sheer cliff in order to escape a monstrous pursuer who is threatening our life.

As to how I found myself back at our workshop, I am unable to provide precise information. Some of my fellow pupils said that I had lost my way through fear, others that I had lost my senses into the bargain. I let them make their jokes. Only when those who had taken packages to the palace before me stood up and began to gabble that they too had eaten sweets from the round cupboard which revolved on a pivot, and that the room with which it communicated as it turned was not the *salon* or the bed-chamber of the princess, but the harem larder, and that the sweet voice belonged not to my beloved princess but to the ancient palace eunuch – only then did my sense of pride rebel, and I started a quarrel with all of them which led to such a coolness between us that I never spoke to them from that day forth.

It goes without saying that I never set foot in the harem again; for not only was I saddened by the thought that my princess was pining away behind the round cupboard on the shores of the Bosporus, but I was perplexed that she did not send her father to ask me to become her husband, as did all the princesses whom my grandfather had known.

After this sad disappointment, the dull and unattractive routine of practical life and the difficulties of the beginner in learning his trade seemed to me to be twice or thrice as burdensome. I began to be oppressed by their weight and to become sickly in the prison-like atmosphere of the Stambul Bazaar, behind the iron gates of the Kebedji Khan, to whose lead-roofed vaults I directed not the charming strains of love songs, but the weeping and wailing of the childish homesickness that gnawed at my heart.

Above all I began to loathe my master, a wizened, sickly old man who, while accompanying the noisy chewing of his voracious scissors with ridiculous movements of his toothless jaws, never ceased to observe me over his huge round spectacles, lest I might stretch my benumbed legs or straighten for a moment my exhausted spinal column.

One day, either through weakness or through obstinacy, I persisted in breaking this sacred rule of tailoring decorum to such an extent that I had the pleasure of being introduced to the "dumb mistress", in other words the measuring stick that the master kept by his side. This inflamed my indignation to the point of impiety. I remember full well that during this period of obstinacy I began to bewail my fate and blame God for having had the bright idea of sewing that famous leather robe with His own hands to clothe Eve's nakedness, thus inaugurating the tailor's profession. If I

were God, I said to myself, I would have left Eve in the state
in which I had created her. What harm would the poor
woman have done me, naked as she was? Indeed, I believe
she would have been even more beautiful. As long as God
kept the woman in Paradise, that is, in His own home, He
left her naked; but when He decided to offload her for ever
on to poor Adam and to send her out into the world, He
endowed her with an ornament. What harm He did in so
doing! He personally founded the wretched guild of tailors,
condemning me to sit here cross-legged and bent over from
dawn to deepest night, and instituted the lamentable custom according to which fathers, when marrying off their
daughters, give them as their dowries not inner virtues, in
so far as they have such things at home, but outer luxuries.

I am certain that I would have formulated these last
pedantic details more simply then, had not a familiar voice
called my name from below, thus interrupting my mournful train of thought before it definitively took on a logical
form.

Despite my mother's repeated admonitions that a trade
is a golden bracelet which I must obtain at all costs – that
a rolling stone gathers no moss, and suchlike – I had persisted in sending messages (I did not yet know how to write
then), beseeching her to recall me and set me to learn a
more tolerable trade. Although I had little probability of
success, I at least hoped to be rid of this master and to
breathe the freer and fresher atmosphere outside the
Bazaar and the khans. Above all I had a secret desire to
serve with the chief tailor of the Sultan's harem at the
Dolmabahche Palace who lived on the Asian shore of the
Bosporus, opposite the palace. There, I thought to myself,

the princesses would hear me singing and would either get
into their rowing-boat and come to me or else beckon to
me from the window to swim to them. Clearly, despite my
experiences, I could not rid my mind of the princess; for,
as I have said, I had utter confidence in my grandfather's
words. He was the most travelled, the most experienced
man I knew. And if I did not manage to bag a princess here
in Constantinople, grandfather would eventually advise me
where to find those princesses who fall in love with tailor-
boys. Because there could be no doubt but that he had seen
them and met them; it may be that he had fallen in love
with one of them, even though the poor fellow was neither
a tailor nor a particularly good singer.

Thus, when I heard that voice calling my name, I leapt
with exultation, for it was the voice of Thymios, my grandfather's servant.

The room in which we worked was a small attic constructed, like a swallow's nest, high up between two domed
arches which formed the top of the stone arcades built
round the central courtyard of the khan. This attic was
reached from the arcade by a narrow ladder, the top of
which rested against the very floor on which we used to sit
working. A moment after I heard my name, Thymios' head
appeared behind the rotten rungs of the ladder. My premonition was right: Thymios' earnest eyes were searching for
one of the students. I did not need him to call me; I did not
need him to finish climbing the ladder in order to be convinced that my senses were not deceiving me. I sprang up
from my place like a captive bird that unexpectedly finds
the door of its cage open.

"Grandpa is 'wrestling with the angel,'" said Thymios

without any preliminaries as he climbed. "Grandpa is dying and he's asking for you. Come, we must hurry. You see, if you don't get there in time, he'll die with his eyes open."

Standing on the landing, Thymios lent additional gravity to his words by beckoning to me like a man who has no time to lose.

I do not know whether it was his words, the tone of his voice, or the seriousness of his look that contributed most to my agitation. I only remember that for some time after Thymios had finished speaking I stood dumbstruck and rooted to the spot, and his words caused shudders of horror to rack my nerves.

Grandfather wrestling with the angel! That was bad enough. But asking for me – that was even worse. That meant that grandfather was unable to handle the angel alone and was summoning me to help him!

This childish thought occurred to me because formerly I used to wrestle with grandfather, climbing on his back and his tall shoulders, especially when I caught him sitting on his cushion by the fire. In those noisy contests grandfather always declared me the winner and always recognized my superiority, introducing me formally to anyone who happened to be present as his *pehlivan*, that is, the professional wrestler that pashas keep ready to wrestle with anyone who boasts of being the strongest man in town; then the wrestler has either to floor him or to hand over his position to him. Since I had formerly held this title with such pride, I thought it quite natural that, being unable to defeat the angel himself, grandfather should summon me, his *pehlivan*, to help him hurl his opponent to the ground, or even to undertake this fearful life-and-death struggle single-handed.

But how could I go through with it? Where would I wrestle with the angel? On the couch by the fire or on the marble threshing-floor? No, no, no! I'm afraid! I can't do it!

My knees were knocking with fear, and I was inclined to sit down again in my place, when I suddenly realized that this was my only chance not only to escape the clutches of my master, but also to ask my grandfather, while there was still time, where in the world he had met the princesses about whom he spoke as if he had eaten and drunk and conversed with them.

But what about the master? What's he going to say? Will he let me go? Is he going to let me escape after assuring us not an hour ago that all his apprentices are his inalienable property? How frightful! I should have thought of that in the first place!

As soon as Thymios had come to our room, the master dropped his scissors with a clatter on to his counter and, raising his huge spectacles from his eyes on to his wrinkled forehead, sat defiantly with his hands resting on his thighs, darting threatening glances at this man who had dared to trespass on the tyrant's domain without following the requisite protocol. My fellow pupils were all clearly moved, but none of them dared stir or even straighten up. All these things were bad omens. Certainly he would not let me leave.

"His grandfather is wrestling with the angel!" Thymios told him, pulling an even longer face than before. "His grandfather is leaving this world and wants to see the boy. It's his last wish, you know."

The master, whose rage seemed to be at its height, was already opening his trembling lips to curse, as he used to do during his violent outbursts of anger, but Thymios' last phrase, uttered with a certain mysterious piety and with a strangely altered tone of voice, acted like magic upon the inhuman old man. His agitated features immediately became calm, his defiant stance was relaxed and, with a kindness that I had never seen in him before, he held out his hand for me to kiss. This was his permission to leave.

My confusion and inexperience led me to believe at that moment that Thymios, who was able to tame my grandfather's unruly bulls with his stentorian voice and his iron hands, also had the power to chant spells from afar and to pacify my even fiercer master. Now, however, I attribute this unexpected change to that religious respect which is due to the dying.

It is indeed to be wondered at how even the most troublesome of men become respectful and eager to obey the last wish of the dying. I do not know if it is believed that those who hinder the fulfilment of this wish bring down upon themselves the disfavour of heaven. Perhaps – in keeping with the wisdom of popular morality – each man avoids doing what he does not wish to be done to him. It is none the less certain that so long as it still has an unfulfilled wish, the departing soul is unable to tear itself away from the body which is now alien to it, and instead of abandoning it completely it hovers moaning and groaning on the lips of the dying man. It is considered frightful and impious for the friends and relations not to hasten to perform whatever it is in their power to do, in order to prepare a quiet and pleasant departure for the soul from a world to which it no longer belongs but to which it is still tied by its last wish. From the facial expression of the dead person, after he has given up the ghost, one can conclude without a doubt whether or not this had occurred.

Thus it happens that moving and sometimes heart-rending scenes take place at the bedsides of the dying. Here the prodigal son and the thoughtless daughter, whose frivolous behaviour has enraged their strict father, thus banishing them from the bosom of the family, are commended by the now frail mother to the indulgence of the father, who embraces them lovingly amid the abundant tears of all present. Here the stepmother, a figure hated since time immemorial among the Greeks, entrusted by the dying father to the loving care of the child he has had by his former wife, receives from the stepson the most devoted attentions. Here long-standing family disagreements are reconciled; festering hatreds between brothers are expunged; and even mortal enmities between relatives are dissolved. And here even the distant members of the family gather together for the same purpose from all corners of the land, not in malicious and impious expectation of material gain but because their souls, attached by nature more closely to the departing spirit, are instinctively drawn to meet it once again while it is still near them in the world, and to exchange with it their last spiritual kiss. For, as is plain to see, the soul that flies up amid their blessing and good wishes goes to meet the members of the family who have already died. Thus this partial separation becomes a general meeting with those souls, an indirect communication of the living with the dead. The departing soul will soon find itself in heaven among its loved ones, who will crowd round asking if it has seen their dear ones on earth and how they are. Thus no one who has the slightest respect and affection for his dead should absent himself from the bedside of a dying relative. If one of the relations, whether through illness or through absence abroad, is unable to attend this last meeting, those who are present carefully avoid mentioning his name, lest the sick man might desire to see him. For then, if the relation in question should fail to arrive in time, the dead man's eyes will remain half-closed in anticipation of his arrival well after the life has quite gone out of them.

This was what Thymios meant when he told me that if I did not arrive in time, grandfather would die with his eyes open.

Thus, after my first confusion had passed, when, after taking my leave, I rode through the Adrianople Gate of Constantinople, not on a gold-caparisoned charger, but seated behind Thymios on the hindquarters of my grandfather's lanky horse, clasping with both hands not the fair princess whom I had hoped to take to my father's cottage, but Thymios' red waist-band, for fear of slipping off the lean cruppers of the horse – thus, I thought of nothing, I worried about nothing so much as whether we might not reach the village in time and poor grandfather would die with open eyes.

The old long-legged horse cantered as fast as its double load and the appalling state of the roads allowed. The distance we had to travel was long, and Thymios had left grandfather dying two days earlier. Grandfather could surely not keep up his struggle with the angel for as long as this. His ninety-eight years had long since bowed his manly stature. For sure, the angel would lay poor grandfather out on the ground and he would die with his eyes open!

Thymios, who did not address a word to me except to

ask me every so often whether I was still sitting on the horse's cruppers, seemed to share the same concern as myself, for he never ceased whipping the horse to make it gallop as fast as possible. In these circumstances Thymios was quite likely to make his enquiry without there being anyone on the horse's cruppers to answer him. Fortunately he realized this in time and, untying a portion of his long red waist-band, he wrapped it a couple of times round me and round his own waist. And so, safely attached to him as if I were some inanimate appendage such as country-folk carry in their waist-bands, I continued the fantastic journey, whose impressions I have never forgotten.

It was autumn, and the days were already drawing in. A cold wind blew through the sparse trees of the forest, disturbing the trembling sleep of their half-naked branches from which, mournfully sighing, innumerable leaves were whirling down to the ground. On nights such as this the moon, appearing at intervals from behind murky clouds, enhances the wild melancholy of nature and, instead of providing comfort, fills the wayfarer's heart with vague fears and continuous shudders. The wildness of our progress was increased by the uneven speed with which our tall horse passed by the various objects on either side of the road, before I had time to make out their blurred outlines and thus calm my timorous heart. Thymios' unbroken and portentous silence, the unexpectedness of the journey, the reason why we were travelling and the way we were doing it – with me half hanging on to Thymios' waist-band and half rocking up and down on the back of the horse – all this, while keeping my childish heart in perpetual anxiety, excited my imagination to the point of delirium.

That night I beheld weird conjunctions of clouds carried along one on top of the other by the wind, and I saw them, with the aid of the moonlight and my prejudiced imagination, as a vast pair of wrestlers fighting for their lives. One of them, with his pleated white loincloth fluttering in the wind and with embroidered sleeves on his shirt, was unmistakably my grandfather. The other, with a long flowing mane of hair, with white wings on his shoulders, with a scaly breastplate and with a flaming sword in his bare right hand, was surely the angel: I had seen him so many times on the left-hand door of the sanctuary in our village church. Poor grandfather! How could he possibly grapple with such a fearsome opponent?

Every time that, benumbed by fatigue and the excessive strain on my nerves, I leaned my head to one side and closed my eyes, I dreamed of grandfather laid out on the floor of grandmother's living room, wrapped in the painted shroud that she had brought him from Jerusalem, with the icon of the Saviour on his breast and the yellow candles wedged between the bony fingers of his hands. Fragrant basil, savory, curry plant and whatever other flowers customarily adorn the bodies of old men covered grandfather from the waist down; the censers and two large candles burned high on either side of his head, and between the candles, sitting on a stool, a schoolboy lent forward reading aloud from the psalter and proudly displaying his reward on his shoulder: an embroidered red kerchief knotted at one corner. Grandfather's pillow was half of that which grandmother had so often shown us with pride, telling us that this was the pillow on which she and her lord and master had stood during their wedding about ninety years before. Grandfather's pillow was stuffed with half of the now unrecognizable flowers and blossoms that the congregation had sprinkled over the newlyweds as they left the church. The piercing wails of the keeners, which were capable of moving even the most impassive to tears, presented my grandfather as the best and most virtuous of men. Why then does his head not rest peacefully on the pillow? Why does his face not display that holy serenity, that deeply-dreaming expression which is usually observed in old people who have gone peacefully to eternal rest? A mournful plaint seems to be hovering on his pale lips. Beneath his bushy white eyebrows his eyes shine like clouded glass, open, staring towards the door of the house. Who is he waiting for? Which of his loved ones did the poor man still desire to see when he died with open eyes?...

I awoke, troubled by the horror of the dream. I straightened my aching neck, leaned my head to the other side, and went back to sleep.

It seemed as if a long time had passed since grandfather's death, as if he was by now buried in front of the church. The grave was dug, but grandfather was not lying in it; he was sitting on the ground, leaning against the white stone cross in the moonlight. At the foot of the cross stood a little lamp and a smoking censer; beside it was a small *tsouréki* coated with honey and an earthenware jar of old red wine. But grandfather, with his headdress coiled low around his forehead and his white eyebrows puckered in a frown, seemed dissatisfied with these offerings and had no desire to touch them. Instead, he kept his mournful eyes fixed on the road, looking and looking, as if he were waiting with ever increasing impatience for someone to come. Suddenly, as though his patience were exhausted, grandfather leaped up, standing at his full height, and with him rose the cross on which he had been leaning; but now it was no longer the cross but grandfather's tall white horse, on which I was returning to the village, unsaddled, unbridled, and leaner and wilder than ever. Grandfather jumped on his back and the horse reared frantically in the air, eyes aflame, flared nostrils steaming and mane undulating unevenly. Horse and rider seemed to be galloping towards me with a look of indescribable anger and revenge. But while both were being carried along in the air, I could hear the clatter of the horse's hooves and felt their vibrations as if I were sitting on its back. Grandfather's long headscarf, having come untied, was fluttering in the wind, rendering his appearance so unspeakably frightful that the nearer he rode the more my discomfort increased, the more my heart was gripped with fear, the more my brain reeled and my senses fled. Two or three times I tried to call for help, to beg for mercy, but my voice stuck in my throat. When in supreme anxiety I uttered a loud cry of horror, I felt as if a great millstone had been lifted from my chest. Because – I woke up.

It goes without saying that after such a fright I dared not fall asleep again. Besides, dawn was already approaching and I thought we would soon be reaching the village.

Nevertheless, it was past noon when we dismounted in front of grandfather's house. Without a word, Thymios went off to the stables to see to the exhausted horse. I opened the door silently and entered the low house with its tiled floor. Deep silence reigned throughout the house. But everything around me was unchanged: the same cleanliness throughout as before, the same tidiness, with every household utensil in its proper place, even the broom, adorned with its multicoloured strips of felt. Only grandfather's shoes, which were always dusted and polished, were not standing with their toes towards the front door, outside the room in which he usually spent the day. Their absence made the house look empty, deserted, abandoned. Grandfather was not there! And since I could not suppose that he was away on a journey, a mournful premonition brought the tears to my eyes.

Suddenly, from the back of the house, towards the right where the larder door was open, I heard my grandmother mumbling. I pricked up my ears. Grandmother was grumbling as usual as she put the dishes away, and was giving someone the rough edge of her tongue.

"So you expect me to feed you, eh? You expect me to feed an idler, you lazybones? What did God give you hands for? So you would run around after me all the time? Off with you, go and do some work, you layabout, otherwise there's going to be real ructions!"

From the clattering of her clogs on the flagstones I concluded that she was chasing after someone to carry out her threat. Then the tom-cat ran out of the larder door at full pelt, its tail erect and an expression in its eyes that seemed to say to me, "I should get out now while the going's good!"

Oh, I thought to myself, poor grandfather has died and, for want of anyone to be angry with, grandmother's picking a quarrel with the cat!

Then grandmother appeared, grumbling as always, her arm raised and holding her spindle. I shall never forget the expression on her face and the stance of her body when she saw me so unexpectedly in the house.

"Dearie me!" she exclaimed after a few moments of mute surprise, and, dropping the spindle on the ground, she slapped her knees with both hands. Then, still bent forward with her hands on her knees, she stared at me again in amazement and, with genuine elation, as if she were informing her own heart of the event, she said, "Our little devil's come home!"

I rushed forward to jump into her arms, but grandmother, frowning suddenly, observed me closely as though she were in doubt as to my identity.

"Where have you come from, you rascal?" she said in an admonishing tone. "Where have you come from, eh? From the moon? You're so pale, anyone would think you've taken a dose of Jew's sulphur! For shame! A plague on the witch! Dearie me! Don't just stand there with that hangdog look, grab some water, quickly!"

Picking up two jugs, she held them out to me. Motionless, I took one in each of my numb hands.

I knew that no one ever crossed grandmother's threshold without being pressed into doing some chore or other. Nevertheless, after the way in which I had been summoned from Constantinople, and considering the purpose for which I had come, I expected to be informed what had become of poor grandfather in his struggle with the angel. So I stood there, unwillingly holding the jugs and wondering how to broach the subject, after his wife's behaviour and the reception she had given me.

But grandmother was accustomed to seeing her orders obeyed instantly.

"Don't just stand there, you weakling!" she shouted. "Don't just stand there! Are you afraid of straining your kid-

neys? And to think you want a shirt and collar from me! A
curse on you, you good-for-nothing, you rascal, you lazybones!"

In such circumstances grandmother resembled those
contraptions which, once wound up, must play their music
to the last note. Thus, as soon as she had made these intro-
ductory remarks, I grasped the jugs and hastened off towards the spring. But my obedience was not enough to interrupt her. Grandmother's tongue continued its tune for
I know not how long after my departure, for when I returned she was still mumbling even more vehemently and
needlessly than usual. For this reason, when, having taken
the full jugs from my hands, she replaced them with two
empty ones, I had no thought of tarrying, but ran off towards the spring with great eagerness, hoping in this way
to propitiate her.

"Where's grandpa, grandma?" I asked respectfully, having returned to find her in a better mood, probably because
there was no other task at hand for me to perform.

"And well might you ask!" she exclaimed, tuning herself
up to another key. "He's gone and left me! The layabout,
the lazybones, the good-for-nothing, the ne'er-do-well!"
and so on and so forth.

Grandmother – I thought to myself – must expect grandfather to come out of his tomb every morning to perform
the tasks she assigned to him during his life, and to return
to his grave in the evening!

"What do you expect poor grandpa to be doing now
there's no work to do?" I said in a low voice, as if talking to
myself.

"Why, he's sunning himself!" retorted grandmother,

winding herself up to an even higher pitch. "He's sunning his belly, the idler, the sponger, the laggard!" and so on and so forth.

How strange, I thought. She's keeping her eye on the poor man even in the next world to see what he's up to.

"Where's he sunning his belly, grandma?" I asked timidly, because I supposed her to be capable of knowing whether grandfather was sunning himself in the warmth of Heaven or in the fires of Hell.

"Why, on Baira!" she shouted irritably. "On Baira! You know him! The imbecile, the loafer, the vagabond....!" This time I did not wait for her to finish, but ran out of the house without a word.

Baira is the great rocky hill to the north of grandfather's house. On it stood the acropolis in ancient times but it now supported on its Pelasgian walls the Turkish prefecture and the houses of certain Ottoman nobles, which present a picturesque spectacle with the variety of their colours and styles. These buildings, protecting the southern side of the hill from the north and east winds and receiving and reflecting the free rays of the sun, provide a cosy refuge even in winter.

Whenever grandfather tired of grandmother's invective, he would sneak out and climb that steep rock and sit for hours high up in the sunshine. Grandfather justified his choice of spot by asserting that as well as the warmth he enjoyed the charming panorama of the country from up there. Everyone knew, however, that grandfather used to climb so high because, owing to her rheumatism, it was the only place where grandmother could not come and fetch him home.

It was up there, then, to the highest point of the acropolis, that I hastened to climb and there, in his habitual place, I saw grandfather sitting in the sun with his head-scarf coiled about his head and wearing his snow-white loincloth. (Grandmother allowed him to wear his woollen breeches only at festivals and on her name-day.) Grand-father was holding a stocking – for grandmother, I assume – knitting it with stout box-wood needles, which he was so skilful at making and handling. For a moment I thought I was still dreaming.

But the gravel and earth of the steep slope rolling down under my hastening feet attracted the old man's attention. He recognized me as soon as he raised his eyes from his knitting:

"Yorgi, Yorgi, pudding and pie,
Kissed the girls and made them cry."

This was the rhyme with which the guileless old man always welcomed me with open arms.

This was no illusion. This was no ghost. Grandpa's thrown the angel on the ground and saved his own life! I thought to myself. What joy! What jubilation!

"Have you been to Constantinople, love?" asked grand-father when we had finished embracing and kissing and my tears had ceased to flow. "Have you been to Constantin-ople? Have you seen the world?"

"Yes, grandpa. I saw Sylivria with its great high gate and mills with sails that turn in the wind!"

"Forget that!" said grandfather. "Did you go through the land where the sun bakes bread? Did you see the dog people?"

"No, grandpa, I didn't. Where do the dog people live?"

"Just before you get to the land where the sun bakes bread," answered grandfather, indicating a point on the horizon with his finger, like a geography teacher who is aware of the places he is talking about. "They're men in front," he continued, "and dogs behind. They cajole you from the front and eat you from behind. So it's a good thing you didn't go there, love."

"A very good thing!" said I. "Luckily I went to Constantinople by caique, so they couldn't eat me. You should see the sea, grandpa – full of water up to here – and the caiques in the water go along – shhhhh! shhhhh! – with their sails billowing."

"Forget that!" said grandfather again. "Did you sail past the sea's belly-button and see the water whirling round and round and round like the brine in the copper pot when your grandmother the hadji is turning it, and there's a hole in the middle?"[1]

"No, I didn't see it, grandpa!"

"Oh, my poor dear! You didn't see anything!"

"And where's that, grandpa?"

"It's just before you get to the place where the mermaid lives, Alexander's mother," said grandfather, pointing with his finger towards the horizon. "Now you saw *her*, didn't you?"

"No, grandpa, I didn't."

"Oh, my poor dear," sighed grandfather, "you didn't see anything, anything at all!"

"What's the mermaid like, grandpa?"

---

1. In Islam, a hadji is one who has carried out the Hajj, the pilgrimage to Mecca. The Greek Orthodox Church adopted the same title for those who undertake the pilgrimage to the Jerusalem.

"Like this," explained grandfather, gesturing in such a way as if he had the mermaid in front of him and was giving me an anatomical account of her body. "From the belly-button up she's the most beautiful woman, and from the belly-button down she's the most fearful fish. She lives at the bottom of the sea. But should any ship lose courage as it sails over her, she leaps up – hop! – to the surface and – hoop! – she grabs the ship and stops it. Then she calls the captain and asks him: 'Does King Alexander live and reign?' Three times she asks him, love, and if the captain tells her three times that he lives and reigns, she let him be and goes about her business. But if he tells her he doesn't live, she sinks the ship and drowns him!"

And turning grandmother's stocking upside down and shaking it in such a way that the ball of wool inside fell out, grandfather showed me how ships are wrecked. "So," he added, "it's a good thing you didn't see her, love."

"A very good thing, grandpa! Because how could I have gone to Constantinople if I'd been drowned? You should see how big Constantinople is, grandpa, and what different kinds of people there are there, and *hanums* and prin…"[2]

"Forget that!" grandfather interrupted again, as though I were talking of trite and humdrum matters. "Did you see the place where the marble men live?"

"Where's that, grandpa?"

"Now," said grandfather like a man who is summoning up his memory, "it's deep in a forest. In a cave. If you go in from this side you see all the men who've been turned to marble. There's a witch there who watches men going by

___

2. *Hanum* [Turkish *hanım*]: Turkish lady.

and if she falls in love with one of them she lures him inside and turns him to marble, and she keeps him standing there so he can't escape from her. When she feels like it she takes the water of immortality and pours three drops on the crown of his head and immediately the marble softens and he becomes a man, even more handsome than before. Then she sits and eats and drinks and enjoys herself with him, and when she's had enough she looks him straight in the eye and turns him to marble again. So it's a good thing you didn't see her, love!"

I had never doubted that my grandfather was an experienced and much travelled man. But I myself had just returned from the longest journey possible – after the Holy Sepulchre, that is – namely, the journey to Constantinople. I had seen so many wonderful things: I thought, therefore, that I had brought with me enough material for storytelling to occupy the old man's attention, if not his admiration, for several days. But when I heard him saying "Forget that!" with such disdain and contempt, interrupting my most serious subjects as if they meant nothing to him and replacing them with his own stories, which were so marvellous and unfamiliar to me, I bent beneath the weight of his inexhaustible knowledge of the world and, totally abashed, I dared say no more.

After a long silence, during which I felt grandfather triumphing over my lack of experience, I raised my eyes once more to his.

"You must have made many journeys in your life," I said, mixing admiration with flattery.

Grandfather seemed surprised. Obviously my question was unexpected. For some moments he stared at me like a man silently protesting against some slander. Then he spoke: "Me? It's your grandmother, the hadji, who's made the journeys!"

In the tone of his voice there clearly lay concealed a whole story. But since I showed that I did not understand its significance, grandfather softly filled in the details

"One day – she wasn't a hadji yet – I say to her, 'I've made a vow to go to the festival at Sarakinou, love.'

"'Well, go then,' she says. 'What do I want you here for, eh? What do I want you for? To sit there and keep guard over me.'" And, lowering his voice even more: "'You so-and-so and such-and-such!'" he added expressively.

"'Very well,' she says. 'I'll get everything ready for you.'

"I shaved, got dressed up, saddled the horse, crossed myself and mounted. Then she appears."

Lowering his voice so as to be scarcely audible, grandfather imitated grandmother's turns of phrase:

"'Where do you think you're going, drat you and blast you? Where do you think you're going?'

"'To St Mary's church, love, at Sarakinou.'

"'You mean you're leaving the cow to go to St Mary's? You so-and-so and such-and-such! Are you thinking so much about the festival that you can't spare a thought for the pregnant cow that's in its last week?'

"Now I wanted to talk to her," continued grandfather, resuming his normal tone, "but she wouldn't let me get a word in edgeways. When I saw I wouldn't get anywhere with her, I said:

"'All right, love. I give in.'

"'But what'll people say, after you've made all these preparations and bought candles and oil and incense? And what about the horse? What'll the horse say after you've shod it and saddled it? The horse is raring to go!'"

Grandfather gave me a meaningful wink, expecting me to understand. Finally, having waited in vain, he exclaimed:

"Don't you see what she was getting at? Well, I lifted her up, sat her on the horse and packed her off to the festival with her brother."

"Then what did you do, grandpa?"

"Well, love, I waited behind in the cowshed for the cow to give birth. And in the end the miserable creature didn't calve," he added, as if the animal were to blame for this failure, "but it put a jinx on my journeys, and every time I've set out on a journey since then, some obstacle has got in my way."

"How, grandpa?"

"Oh dear!" he said, not sure how to connect his travelling misadventures with the delayed calving of the cow. "I don't know. But when your grandmother the hadji is mixed up in anything you can't get to the bottom of it. It's quite unbelievable how she managed it, how she fixed it. Every time I've got ready to travel, some animal was giving birth, or the bees were swarming, or someone was ill, or some visitor was expected – it's as if she'd ordered something to turn up just as I'd crossed myself and mounted the horse.

"All these years we've been married, I would make the preparations and she would make the journey. The same happened with Redestos, the same with Sylivria, the same with Midia – the same everywhere. There was one journey I was planning secretly, love. I was keeping it for myself. For years and years I put aside any little extra money and I hid it as best I could. When I'd saved 50,000 piastres, I made up my mind and called you grandmother – when I had my mind made up I didn't stand on ceremony with her. So I say to her with a decisive air, 'Chrousi! I'm planning to go on a journey, so make sure there's no pregnant animal or sick man or anyone needing help, and make sure no visitor enters the house, otherwise I'll smash his legs!'"

Grandfather made a gesture which showed his admiration for what he had done. Then he went on.

"You should have been there to see how flummoxed she was! She didn't say a word! That's just what I wanted. So I sent for the priest and he confessed me; I called your grandmother and signed all my property over to her. I called the villagers and received forgiveness from each of them, because you see, love, a journey is – well, it's the longest journey in the world, it's a matter of life and death!

"The next day I got the horse out and crossed myself ready to mount. Your grandmother – she wasn't a hadji yet – peeped round the door to look at me. I was in high dudgeon, and if she had so much as put the slightest thing in my way, all hell would have broken loose. Your grandmother knew this and didn't say anything. That's just what I wanted. When I had crossed myself ready to mount, I said to her:

"'Come on, Chrousi, it's a matter of life and death! Forgive me and may God forgive you!' Whereupon she burst into tears."

Grandfather spoke agitatedly, as if the scene were taking place at that very moment. Snivelling and attempting as far as he could to reproduce his wife's great sorrow, he said:

"'Oh, would that I'd never been born, poor unfortunate wretch that I am! I'm losing my husband, my companion, my master!'"

As if surprised by these decorative appellations, grand-father continued:

"I wasn't expecting that, love. Come what may, I was de-termined. But when I saw your grandmother – my wife – crying, I lost my nerve. How could I leave her to go to the ends of the earth?

"'I've vowed to make a pilgrimage to the Holy Land, love,' I told her. 'What can I do now? If I don't go we'll be damned.'

"'If you've vowed, husband, then we're man and wife, aren't we? – one flesh. So whether you go or I go it comes to the same.'

"The tears in her eyes!" exclaimed grandfather, chang-ing his tone. "What could I say? I lifted her on to the horse and packed her off to the Holy Land with her brother.

"From then on," said grandfather, brushing the palms of his hands together as if he were dusting them, "I've never tried to make a journey."

"So those great journeys of yours, grandpa, when you went round the world, you made them before you married grandma?"

Grandfather resumed his knitting, a mournful smile on his lips.

"Before I was married off to your grandmother the hadji," he said, lowering his eyes, "I wasn't a boy."

"What were you then, grandpa, a girl?"

"Let's say I was practically a girl, love," answered grand-father with his mournful smile, "since I thought I was one and other people believed it too."

His words affected me strangely. Grandfather held his knitting in his hands, and – for all his manly stature, his carefully shaven face, his moustache jauntily trimmed along the edge of his upper lip – his whole facial expression seemed at that moment to contain much that was effeminate and womanly.

"Why yes, love," said grandfather with a sigh, suddenly becoming pensive. "You live in a golden age now, a golden age! You travel about wherever you like. When all's said and done, love, you know what you are. We lived in bad times, unhappy times! Our mothers used to kneel before the icons, love, and beseech the Virgin Mary either to give them a daughter, or to kill the child they carried in their womb so it wouldn't be born a boy."

"Why, grandpa?"

"Because, every so often," said grandfather, looking more and more sullen, "the janissary band would go out – great big fearsome Turks with tall felt hats and red shoes – and they'd go around the villages armed to the teeth, with the imam in front and the executioner behind, and they'd gather the most handsome of the Christian boys, love, and make them into Moslems."

"Why, grandpa?"

"To make them into janissaries," said the old man indignantly. "To make them like themselves, so they'd come back to the country when they grew up and forget they were Greeks, and slaughter their own parents, and dishonour their own sisters who had drunk the same milk with them.

"That day will ne'er be forgot,
That day will aye be curs'd,
When they came and took the children,
That woeful April the first!"

Grandfather groaned as he recited this verse and wiped away his tears.

"That's why," he continued, "when I was born, love, I was baptized Georgia, which means they gave me a girl's name, just as babies were baptized Konstantinia and Thanasia and Dimitro – all boys with girls' names. And together with the name, they dressed me in girl's clothes.

"In all the years that went by I hardly ever went out of our front door, like the mere girl I thought I was. When I was about ten, my father – God rest his soul – sat me down on a stool, cut off my long plaits and took off my dress, saying:

"'Look here, Georgia, from this day forth you're George, you're a boy; from tomorrow you'll be a man, the husband of your little playmate Chrousi.'

"With that, he dressed me in boy's clothes.

"Next day the musicians arrived with their violins and lutes and I was taken to church and married to your grandmother."

"How was that, grandpa, when you were so young?"

"You may ask," said grandfather, similarly perplexed. "I hadn't even learned how to tie my new shoes, and there I was with a wife to look after! But," he went on, knitting his brow, "it had to be. They couldn't hide me any longer and the Sultan's firman said the janissaries could only take unmarried lads. So I was married with pomp and ceremony, and instead of being taken by some janissary I was taken by your grandmother."

"Do you mean to say, grandpa, that you never made a journey in your whole life – not even before you were married?"

Grandfather was unable to find an answer for a few moments. Then, lowering his eyes rather sheepishly, he said:

"I don't know how to put it, love. Before I got married I did go on a journey, but... well... I didn't get all the way, I didn't complete it."

"How was that, grandpa? When?"

The old man let his knitting fall to the ground and, silently fixing his gaze on the horizon, seemed to be occupying his eyes with the landscape spread out below us. The sky was cloudless, the sun low on the horizon, and the elevated position on which we sat afforded the spectator a vast but nonetheless easily embraced panorama.

Around the edge of the acropolis, immediately beneath our gaze, lay the houses of the town, grouped together irregularly, in whose yards men, women and children could be seen busily garnering their autumn produce in their storehouses. Immediately next to the town were the vegetable gardens, surrounded by old trees which were losing their leaves. The last harvesters were loading their late vegetables on to their wagons, and nearby the burning chaff smouldered on the now deserted threshing floors. Further away, stretched out in a semi-circle over a large radius, lay the arable fields of the district, in which the heavy ears of corn no longer waved like the surface of an undulating golden sea; instead, the flocks and herds, sluggishly returning to the town, grazed freely there, gleaning the last green blades of grass. At the extremity of the horizon the vineyards closed off this vast picture like a high border, these too deserted and abandoned after the grape harvest. The brilliant variety of the last autumnal colours, the multitude of streams traversing the area and the picturesque knots of trees and buildings standing on their banks, the burial mounds of the Odrysians[3] rising like great conical humps not only interrupted the usual monotony of a flat landscape, but provided this endless picture with a wonderful and extraordinary unity and variety.

And yet, before this most delightful spectacle – as I still remember – my heart was seized by a mysterious unease, a sorrowful premonition. It was as if life, which had bloomed with such exuberance on this land, were now slowly but surely retreating towards the inmost recesses of nature, while this brilliance that still remained on the earth's face was but the last, the final smile on the lips of a dying man.

Having occupied himself silently and abstractedly with this spectacle for some time, grandfather fixed his gaze on one of the most distant conical humps near the horizon and pointed to it.

"D'you see that knoll, love?"

"Which one, grandpa?"

"There, the highest of them all, where the face of the earth ends."

"Yes, I can see it; it's as high as the sky, grandpa."

"That's right!" said grandfather, delighted by my answer. "The sky's resting on it, isn't it?"

"Yes, grandpa! It's where the earth ends and the sky begins."

"That's right!" exclaimed the old man, even more delighted. Then he fixed me with a proud look. "I managed to get as far as that!"

---

3. An ancient Thracian people, once ruled, according to legend, by Orpheus.

He spoke with such a proud air that I did not know if he meant that he had managed to get as far as the sky, or as far as the knoll that appeared to be supporting the sky.

Grandfather continued:

"You can see the knoll from our window: ever since I was a little child I used to see it, and I had a great yen to go over there and climb to the top of it and enter the heavens. But the trouble was, I was a girl! How could I go out into the street?

"When my father cut my hair and put boy's shoes on me, and made me into a boy in a trice, people were cutting strips of paper and making the marriage garlands, and I sidled out into the yard. The only thing I could think of was the journey."

After a pause, during which grandfather seemed to be collecting his memories, he resumed:

"Outside the chicken-house stood a piece of wood with rungs nailed across it for the chickens to climb up to their roosting places. I'd had my eye on that from the beginning. I'll prop it up against the glass of the sky, I thought, like a ladder, then I'll make a hole in it and climb through. So then, I put this piece of wood over my shoulder, and if anyone saw me they could do what they liked!

"I walked out of the yard, turned right, and off I went! The people who saw me didn't recognize me as Georgia, Syrmas' daughter. It was the first time I'd come out into the outside world.

"Even Chrousi, your grandmother, seeing me like that in my boy's shoes, started throwing stones at me. Not that she recognized me, just that she always used to torment boys. I went on my way. Who could stop me from going on such a journey? I passed by the gardens and the fields, I crossed the river with my eyes fixed on the knoll, and on I went. I went a mile, then two. But what d'you think happened? The more I went on, the further away the knoll seemed to be. The nearer I got, the higher the sky rose up. Well, love, that took the wind out of my sails! I'd already been feeling tired for some time, but I didn't realize it until I saw the edge of the sky was gradually getting further away from the knoll where I was counting on reaching it. Then I lost heart and I realized I felt tired and hungry, the wood I was carrying was like lead, it had begun to get dark and… well… then I turned back and left the journey unfinished.

"Because, you see," the old man added, "I thought of my father among other things. He – God rest his soul – wasn't like your grandmother, the hadji."

"What do you mean, grandpa?"

"Well," he said with a knowing smile, "your grandmother's bark is worse than her bite, but my father's bite was worse than his bark. That's why I turned back. That was the one and only journey of my life," he added pensively, "and I didn't complete it."

"And what about all those things you've seen and know so much about, grandpa?" I asked, greatly perplexed. "When did you go to the land where the sun bakes bread, near where the dog people live?"

"Oh," he replied," I didn't go there; my grandmother told me about it when she was teaching me to knit."

"And didn't you go to the sea's belly-button, grandpa, where the mermaid comes out and grabs the ships and asks them about King Alexander?"

"No, love. My grandmother told me about that too."

"And you didn't go to the cave, grandpa, with the witch who turns men to marble?"

"No, love, it was my grandmother who told me about it."

I cannot describe my increasing disappointment at his every response. So all my great ideas about grandfather's travels, all my respect and trust in him on account of his worldly wisdom and experience suddenly seemed to be founded on stories, on fairy-tales that he had heard from his grandmother at a time when the poor man was so naïve as to believe that he was a female rather than a male! My heart was seized with despair and indignation.

"And the princesses, grandpa, didn't you ever set eyes on them? Didn't you eat and talk with them?"

"What princesses, love?"

"You know, the ones that fall in love with tailor-boys and fall ill and send their father, the king wearing his crown, to go and ask them to be his sons-in-law. Don't you remember telling me? Don't you remember the golden-haired Fairy Queen and the fairies clothed in white that sing and laugh and joke and sew the wedding garments without a single stitch?"

"Oh, yes!" said the old man sadly. "I heard that story too from my grandmother when she was teaching me to embroider and sew. D'you know, love, I don't think even she set eyes on them."

This swept away the last of my illusions! It was not the princess who was waiting for me in the Validé Sultana's harem, behind the round cupboard in the wall! And it was not she who had given me those fragrant sweets, but I know not what filthy, wrinkled, thick-lipped old eunuch! My fellow pupils were right.

Not only this, but all the trials and tribulations I had suffered and was about to suffer, in the sweet hope of returning to the village with a princess at my side, had all been wasted; they were all for nothing. Very well, grandfather, if you ever see me pick up a needle again, tell me I'm a female and don't know it!

I was about to utter this last thought, blaming my grandfather for being the cause of my going to Constantinople and suffering hardship to no avail; but when, raising my eyes, I saw him with his dreamy gaze permanently fixed far away on the top of that conical hump, from which he had once hoped to enter the heavens, some mysterious power froze my voice on my lips.

The sun had sunk much further towards its setting. Every creature, every manifestation of life was withdrawing silently and slowly into the interior of the town. The appearance of the landscape now seemed to me more melancholy, more mournful. My heart was troubled again. How much similarity, how close a relation there was between the physiognomy of the scene below us and the expression on grandfather's pale, withered face, lit by the last rays of the sun!

Poor grandfather! I thought to myself, he wrestled with the angel and beat him without my help, but he exhausted himself and became so weak that no one will be able to save him if he is felled again.

"It's beginning to get cold, love," said the old man suddenly. "Let's go."

Without a word I offered him my arm and, supporting him as best I could, I accompanied him home.

That night was indeed very cold, and next morning a thick frost lay over the withered leaves that covered the

ground in our garden. As soon as I awoke I ran to my
beloved grandfather's house. What a change had occurred
overnight! A silent, grave crowd of relations and neighbours were crowded together in the yard and in grandmother's sitting room, in the middle of which was grandfather, laid out on his back. He seemed not to have woken
yet. On his face was an expression of profound serenity. A
glimmer of other-worldly light, in the form of a gradually
fading smile, played round his features.

Grandmother, with her hands clasped round her knees,
her hopeless gaze fixed on grandfather's face, sat by his side,
pale and motionless as if she were turned to stone. What
would the unfortunate woman not have given to prevent
him from going on this journey! For grandfather's smile
was the gleam of light which his soul was leaving behind
as it departed to heaven.

At last poor grandfather was truly completing the one
and only journey of his life.

My mother's sin

Annio was the only sister we had. She was the darling of our small family. We all loved her, but our mother loved her more than anyone. At table mother always used to sit Annio beside her and give her the best of what we had: whereas she dressed us in our late father's clothes, she would usually buy new ones for Annio. Mother did not even force her into education: whenever she felt like it she would go to school, but if not she stayed at home, a freedom that was not granted to us on any account.

Such exceptions might have been expected to excite unwholesome jealousies among children, especially ones as young as my two brothers and I were at the time when these things occurred. But we knew that deep down our mother's affection was impartial and equal towards all her children. We were certain that these exceptions were but the external manifestations of a natural favour towards the only girl in our household, and we not only tolerated without complaint the attentions that were shown her, but even did our best to increase them.

Sadly Annio, as well as being our only sister, had always been a delicate and sickly child. Even the last-born of the family, who, having been born posthumously, had a better claim than anyone to maternal caresses, conceded his rights to our sister all the more gladly since Annio became neither domineering nor arrogant on this account. On the contrary, she was amiable towards us and loved us all passionately. And, strangely, the girl's tenderness towards us grew rather than decreased as her illness proceeded.

I remember her large, black eyes and her arched eyebrows, which looked ever blacker as her face became paler, a face which was by nature sad and dreamy and on which appeared a gentle look of gaiety only when she saw us all gathered around her. When the neighbours brought her fruit, as one does with invalids, she would usually keep it under her pillow and share it out among us when we came home from school. But she always did this secretly, for otherwise our mother would be angry at our devouring what she would have liked her sick daughter to eat.

As Annio's illness continued to worsen, our mother's attentions were more and more directed towards her. She had not left the house since our father's death, for she had been widowed very young and she was ashamed of taking advantage of the freedom which, even in Turkey, is granted to all mothers of large families. But from the first day that Annio became totally bed-ridden she cast her shame aside. If anyone had had a similar illness, mother would run and ask them how they had been cured. Were some old woman to be secreting herbs with miraculous medicinal properties, mother would hasten to acquire them. Should a traveller pass by with strange appearance and a reputation for learning, she did not hesitate to seek his opinion; for, to simple folk, educated people are omniscient, and under the guise of a poor wayfarer there is sometimes concealed a being endowed with supernatural powers.

The fat neighbourhood barber used to visit us, uninvited but tactfully: he was the only official doctor in the area. As soon as I caught sight of him, I had to run to the grocer's, since he never approached a patient without having gulped down at least a quarter-pint of *raki*.

"I'm old, my dear," he would tell our impatient mother, "I'm old, and if I don't have a swig I can't see properly."

And indeed, he seemed to be telling the truth; for the more he drank, the better able was he to discern which was the fattest hen in our yard and to help himself to it as he left. Although my mother had stopped employing his remedies, she still paid him regularly and without complaint, partly because she did not wish to displease him, and partly because he would often comfort her by asserting that the progress of the illness was satisfactory, and exactly as science would expect from his prescriptions.

This last claim was sadly all too true. Annio's condition was slowly and imperceptibly changing for the worse, and this prolongation of her vague sickness put my mother at her wits' end. If it is to be considered a natural malady, every disease unknown to the folk must either retreat before the rudimentary medical knowledge of the region, or lead to an early death. If it should linger, it is attributed to supernatural causes and described as "demonic": the patient has stopped at some evil place, he has crossed a river at night, when the invisible water-spirits were performing their unnatural rites, or he has crossed paths with a black cat, the metamorphosis of the Evil One.

My mother was more pious than superstitious. At first

she eschewed such diagnoses and refused to employ the spells that were suggested to her for fear of committing a sin. Besides, the priest had already taken the precaution of exorcising the sick girl. But soon she changed her mind. The patient's condition was deteriorating, and motherly love conquered the fear of sin. Religion had to be reconciled with superstition.

Next to the cross on Annio's breast she hung a talisman with mysterious Arabic words on it. Sprinklings with holy water gave way to spells, and the priest's prayer-book was succeeded by witches' incantations. But all this was in vain. The child was becoming progressively worse and my mother was beginning to be unrecognizable. It was as if she had forgotten she had any other children. She no longer sought to know who was feeding us boys, who was washing us and mending our clothes.

An old woman from Sophides, for many years a retainer in our house, cared for us insofar as her great age permitted. There were times when we did not see our mother for days on end. Sometimes she would go and tie a strip of cloth from Annio's dress at some miraculous place in the hope that the illness unfortunately would become tied far away from the girl; sometimes she would repair to neighbouring churches whose saint's day was being celebrated, bearing a yellow candle, equal in length to the height of the sick girl, which she had made with her own hands. But all this proved fruitless. Our poor sister's illness was incurable.

When all other means had been exhausted and all remedies tried, we sought refuge in the last resort for such circumstances. My mother lifted the pining girl in her arms and took her to the church. My elder brother and I followed, carrying the bedding. There, on the cold damp flagstones before the icon of the Virgin Mary, we laid the sweetest object of our cares, our only sister.

Everyone said she had a demon. My mother no longer doubted this and even the sick child had begun to realize it. Thus she had to remain in the church for forty days and forty nights, in front of the holy altar and before the Mother of the Saviour, entrusted solely to their mercy, so as to be saved from the satanic sickness that lurked inside her and pitilessly gnawed at her fragile body. Forty days and forty nights is the limit to which the fearful tenacity of demons can withstand the invisible war waged against them by divine grace. After this term evil is defeated and retreats in shame. Stories are told of the afflicted feeling within their organism the fearful writhings of the final battle, and seeing their enemy fleeing in strange guise, especially when the sacraments are being carried past or when a certain hymn is being chanted. Happy are they who possess sufficient strength to withstand the shock of this struggle. The weak are crushed under the magnitude of the miracle that is taking place within them. But they have no regrets, for if they lose their lives, they gain something more precious: they save their souls.

Such a contingency caused our mother to feel no less anxiety, and no sooner had she placed Annio in position than she began to inquire solicitously how she felt. The sanctity of the place, the sight of the icons and the fragrance of the incense seemed to have a beneficial effect on her spirits for, after the first moments had passed, she livened up and began joking with us.

"Which of the two do you want to play with?" my mother asked her tenderly, "Christakis or Yorgis?"

The sick child threw her an expressive sidelong glance and, as if chiding her for her neglect of us, replied slowly and deliberately:

"Which of the two do I want? I don't want either without the other. I want all the brothers I've got."

My mother drew back and fell silent. After a while she brought our youngest brother into the church, but only for that first day.

In the evening she sent the other two away and kept me alone with her. I still remember the impression that first all-night vigil in the church made on my childish imagination. The dim light of the lamps in front of the icon-screen, scarcely sufficient to illuminate it and the steps in front of it, made the surrounding darkness even more eerie and fearsome than if we had been in complete darkness. Each time a little lamp-flame flickered, it seemed as though the saint on the icon opposite had begun to come to life and to shift about in an effort to break away from the wood and step down to the floor in his voluminous red robes, his halo round his head and his staring eyes set in his pale, impassive face. Every time the chill wind whistled through the high windows, rattling the small panes, I thought the dead buried around the church were climbing the walls and attempting to enter. Trembling with fear, I occasionally saw a skeleton stretching out its fleshless hands to warm them over the brazier that burned in front of us.

Nevertheless, I dared not display the slightest unease, for I loved my sister and considered it a great favour to be constantly near her and near my mother, who would cer-

tainly have packed me off home had she so much as sus-
pected that I was afraid. And so, during the ensuing nights,
I suffered the same shudders with enforced stoicism and
carried out my duties willingly in an attempt to be as com-
plaisant as possible. I would light a fire, bring water and
sweep the church on ordinary days. On Sundays and feast-
days, during matins, I would help my sister stand under
the bible as the celebrant read from it at the sanctuary door.
During the liturgy I would spread the rug on which the
sick girl lay prone while the sacraments were carried over
her. At the end of the service I would bring her pillow in
front of the left-hand door of the sanctuary for her to kneel
there until the priest had disrobed over her and made the
sign of the cross over her face with the Lance, whispering
the hymn, "By the crucifixion, O Christ, the tyranny of the
Great Enemy is abolished, and his power is laid low."

In all this my poor sister followed me with slow, shaky
steps and pale, sad visage, attracting the pity of the congregation and their wishes for her recovery; a recovery
which, sadly, was continually postponed. On the contrary,
the cold and the damp, the strangeness and (I must confess) the awesome nature of her overnight stays in the
church were not slow to take their toll on the patient,
whose condition now began to inspire the utmost fear.
Realizing this, mother began, even in the church, to display
a pitiful indifference towards everything except her daughter. She opened her lips to no one but Annio and the saints
to whom she prayed.

One day I approached her unobserved while she knelt
weeping before the icon of the Saviour.

"Take whichever you want," she was saying, "only leave

me my daughter. But I see that it is to be. You've remembered my sin and you're set on taking my child so as to punish me. Thank you, Lord!"

After some moments of complete silence, during which her tears could be heard falling on the flagstones, she sighed from the bottom of her heart, hesitated a little, then added:

"I've brought two of my children to your feet. Let me keep the girl!"

On hearing these words I felt an icy shudder run through my nerves and my ears began to ring. I could hear no more. When I saw my mother, weighed down by her fearful anxiety, fall motionless on the marble floor, instead of running to her aid I took the opportunity to run out of the church, beside myself and yelling as if Death made visible were threatening to snatch me away.

My teeth were chattering with terror, while I kept on running and running. Without realizing where I was going, I suddenly found myself at a considerable distance from the church. Only then did I stop to regain my breath and dare to turn and look behind me. No one was pursuing me.

I began to recover gradually and to ponder. I recalled all my tendernesses and endearments towards my mother. I tried to remember whether I had ever done her wrong, whether she had anything to reproach me with, but I could not. I began to realize that, ever since that sister of ours was born, far from being loved as I would have wished, I felt rejected. I remembered – and I now seemed to understand why – that my father used to call me his "poor wronged child". Overcome by grief, I began crying. "My mother doesn't love me and doesn't want me!" I said to myself. "I'm not going back to the church ever again!" And I made off towards our house in sorrow and dejection.

My mother soon followed me with my sister, since the priest who, disturbed by my cries, had entered the church and seen the girl, had advised my mother to move her back.

"God is great, my daughter," he told her, "and his grace reaches throughout the world. If he is to cure your child, he will cure her just as well at home."

Unhappy the mother who heard him! For these are the typical words with which priests are wont to send away the dying, lest they expire in the church and defile the sanctity of the place.

When I saw my mother again, she was more downcast than ever but treated me with special fondness and consideration. She took me in her arms, caressed me and kissed me tenderly and repeatedly. It was as if she were trying to appease me. Nevertheless I was unable to eat or sleep that night. I lay on my pallet with half-closed eyes, but kept my ears carefully attuned to any movement from my mother who, as always, kept vigil by the sick girl's bedside. It must have been about midnight when she began pacing about the room. I thought she was preparing to go to bed, but I was mistaken, for in a while she sat down and began keening in a low voice. It was a dirge for our father. Before Annio became ill she used to sing it frequently, but this was the first time I had heard it since the illness began.

This dirge had been composed on the death of my father at her request by a ragged, weatherbeaten Gipsy who was renowned in our district for his skill in improvising verses. I can still see his greasy black hair, his small fiery

eyes and his shaggy chest as he sat inside our front gate surrounded by the copper pots he had collected for tinplating
and, leaning his head on one side, accompanied his mournful song with the plaintive notes of his three-stringed lyre.
My mother stood in front of him holding Annio and listened in tears, while I held on tightly to her dress and hid
my face in its folds because, for all the sweetness of the
notes, the wild singer's face looked so fearsome to me.

When my mother had learned her sad lesson, she untied two silver coins from her headscarf and gave them to
the Gipsy – we still had plenty of them then. Then she
served him bread and wine and whatever other food she
had to hand. While he was eating down below, my mother
went upstairs and repeated the elegy to herself so as to fix
it in her memory. She seemed to find it beautiful for, just
as the traveller was leaving, she ran after him and presented him with a pair of my father's baggy trousers.

"God forgive your husband, sister!" cried the bard in
amazement and, loading his copper utensils on his back,
left our courtyard.

This, then, was the lament that my mother was singing
that night. I listened to it and let my tears flow silently, but
I dared not move. Suddenly I smelled the fragrance of incense.

"Oh," I said, "our poor Annio is dead!" And I leapt out
of bed. Before me a bizarre scene was being enacted. The
sick girl was breathing heavily, as always. Next to her had
been placed a man's suit, laid out as if ready to be worn. To
the right was a stool covered with a black cloth, on which
stood a bowl of water with a lighted candle on either side.
My mother was on her knees censing these objects, her

attention fixed on the surface of the water. I must have
blanched with fear for, when she saw me, she hastened to
reassure me.

"Don't be afraid, my little child," she said mysteriously.
"These are your father's clothes. Come, you too must ask
him to come and cure our Annio."

She made me kneel next to her.

"Come, father, and take me away so that Annio will get
well," I exclaimed, my words interrupted by my sobs. I
looked reproachfully at my mother to show her that I knew
she was asking that I should die instead of my sister.
Foolishly, I did not realize that in this way I was heighten-
ing her despair. But I believe she forgave me: I was very
young then and could not understand her feelings.

After a few moments of complete silence she again
censed the objects in front of us and fixed her whole attention on the water in the wide bowl on the stool. Suddenly
a little moth, circling above it, touched it with its wings and
slightly ruffled its surface. My mother bent forward de-
voutly and crossed herself, just as when the sacraments are
carried past in church.

"Cross yourself, my child," she whispered, deeply moved
and not daring to raise her eyes.

I obeyed mechanically. When the little moth disap-
peared into the dark depths of the room, my mother
breathed again and stood up, looking gratified and cheer-
ful.

"Your father's soul has passed by," she said, still following the flight of the moth with a look of affection and devotion. Then she drank some of the water and gave me
some to drink. Then it occurred to me that formerly she

used to give us water to drink from that bowl as soon as we awoke. I remember that whenever my mother did this she was bright and joyful all day, as if she had been vouchsafed some great but secret bliss.

When I had drunk, she went over to Annio's pallet with the bowl in her hands. The girl was not asleep, but neither was she completely awake. Her eyelids were half-closed; her eyes, inasmuch as they were visible, emitted a strange gleam through their thick black lashes. My mother carefully raised the girl's slender body and, while with one hand she supported her back, with the other she offered the bowl to her wasted lips.

"Come, my love," she said. "Drink this water, it will make you better."

The patient did not open her eyes, but seemed to hear the voice and understand the words. Her lips broadened into a sweet smile of tenderness. Then she drank down a few drops of that water, which was indeed to cure her. For as soon as she swallowed it she opened her eyes and tried to breathe. A slight groan escaped her lips, and she fell back heavily against my mother's arm.

Our poor Annio! She had been relieved of her torments.

Many people had criticized my mother for simply shedding abundant but silent tears over my father's body, while women who were unrelated to him lamented vociferously. The unfortunate woman did this for fear that her actions might be misconstrued, that she might go beyond the bounds of the decorum that befitted young women – for, as I have said, my mother was widowed at a very early age.

When our sister died, my mother hardly gave a thought now to what people would say about her heartrending laments. The whole neighbourhood was aroused and came to comfort her, but her mourning was fearful and inconsolable.

"She'll lose her senses," whispered those who saw her, bent double, lamenting between the graves of our sister and our father.

"They'll be left to their fate," said those who met us in the street, abandoned and uncared for. The passage of time and the admonitions and reprimands of the church were required to make her come to her senses, remember her surviving children and resume her domestic duties. It was then that she noticed where our sister's long illness had left us.

All our savings had gone to pay for doctors and remedies. She had sold a large number of rugs – her own handiwork – for trifling sums, or had given them as payment to sorcerers and enchantresses. Others had been stolen from us by these and their kind, who had taken advantage of the lack of surveillance that prevailed in our house. On top of this, our supplies of animal fodder were exhausted and we no longer had any livelihood.

Far from dismaying my mother, however, this gave her twice the energy she had possessed before Annio became ill. She moderated, or rather concealed, her mourning; she overcame the timidity of her age and sex and, taking the gardening fork in her hands, began to work in other people's gardens as though she had never known a life of comfort and independence.

For a long time she supported us by the sweat of her

brow. The wages were paltry and our needs were great, yet she did not allow any of us to help her in her work. Plans for our future would be made and reviewed every evening by the fire. My elder brother was to learn our father's trade so as to take his place in the family. I had – or rather wished – to leave home to find a job, and so on and so forth. But before all this could happen, we all had to finish our education; for, as mother used to say, an uneducated man is like an unhewn log.

Our financial hardships reached a peak when the area suffered a drought and the prices of provisions rose. But instead of giving up hope of our upkeep, mother added to our number a girl whom, after long efforts, she succeeded in adopting.

This event changed the austere and monotonous nature of our family life, and once more introduced a certain vitality into it. Right from the start this adoption was a cause for celebration. My mother put on her festive clothes and led us to the church, clean and well-kempt, as though we were to take Communion. After the liturgy we all stood before the icon of Christ where, amid the surrounding throng and in the presence of her natural parents, my mother took her adopted daughter from the priest's hands after having first sworn, in the hearing of all those assembled, to love and to nurture her as though she were flesh of her flesh.

Our adoptive sister's entry into our household took place in a no less imposing and triumphal manner. The village elder and my mother went ahead with the girl, while we walked behind. Our relatives and those of our new sister followed us to our front gate, where the elder lifted the girl up high and displayed her for a few moments in front of the assembled people. Then, in a loud voice, he asked:

"Which of you is more a parent or relative of this child than Despinio Michaliessa and her family?"

The girl's father was pale and gazed sorrowfully in front of him. His wife leaned on his shoulder, weeping. My mother trembled with fear lest anyone should shout "I am" and thus thwart her happiness. But no one answered. So the child's parents kissed it for the last time and went away with their relatives, while our relations went in with the elder and were entertained by us.

From that moment our mother began to lavish more attention on our adoptive sister than perhaps we were ever vouchsafed at her age in far more fortunate times. While I was soon wandering homesick in a distant land and my brothers were slaving away from morning till night in the workshops, the stranger was lording it over our house as if it were her own.

My brothers' low wages would have been sufficient to relieve mother of her work; but, instead of spending the money so that she could relax, she used it to build up a dowry for her adopted daughter and continued working for her living. I was far, far away, and for many years I was unaware of what was happening at home. Before I could manage to return home, the cuckoo in our nest had grown up, received a dowry and married as if she was truly a member of our family.

Her wedding which, it seems, was deliberately celebrated rather precipitately, was a joyous occasion for my unfortunate brothers who, relieved of the additional burden, were able to breathe again. They were right to rejoice for, as well as having never felt any sisterly affection for them, the girl eventually displayed her ingratitude towards the woman who had looked after her with such loving care as few legitimate sons and daughters have known. Thus my brothers had reason to be pleased and to believe that my mother had been taught her lesson.

How great was their surprise, therefore, when a few days after the wedding they saw her coming home, tenderly clasping to her breast a second baby girl, this time still in swaddling-clothes!

"Poor mite!" exclaimed my mother, leaning compassionately over the infant's face. "It wasn't enough for it to lose its father before it was born, but its mother died too and left it without a roof over its head."

Deriving a certain satisfaction from this unfortunate concurrence of circumstances, she triumphantly displayed her trophy to my dumbfounded brothers. Their filial devotion was considerable and my mother's authority great, but my poor brothers were so dismayed that they could not stop themselves suggesting politely to their mother that she would do well to abandon her intentions. Finding her adamant, however, they openly declared their displeasure and denied her the management of their financial affairs. But all in vain.

"Don't bring me anything," said my mother. "I'm working to feed her just as I fed you. When my Yorgis comes back home he'll provide her with a dowry and find a husband for her. Have no fear! My son promised me: 'I'll feed you, mother, both you and your foster-daughter.' Yes, that's what he said, bless him!"

Yorgis was me. I had indeed made this promise, but long

before, when our mother was working to feed our first adoptive sister as well as us. I used to keep mother company during breaks from my lessons, playing nearby while she was digging or weeding. One day we broke off from work and returned from the fields to escape the unbearable heat, from which my mother had almost fainted. On the way home we were caught in a violent downpour, such as usually happens in our parts after an excessive heat-wave. We were not far from the village, but we were obliged to cross a torrent that was pouring down violently in full flood. My mother offered to carry me on her shoulders, but I refused.

"You're weak from exhaustion," I told her. "You'll throw me in the river."

I hitched up my clothes and ran into the stream before she could restrain me. I had placed more trust in my abilities than I should; for, before I could think of retreating, I lost my footing and toppled over, swept along by the torrent like a walnut-shell. All I remember from then on is the piercing shriek uttered by my mother as she threw herself into the stream to save me.

It is a wonder that I was not the cause of her drowning as well as my own, for that torrent had a bad reputation in our parts. When they say of someone that "he got carried away", they mean he was drowned in that very torrent.

My mother, however, faint as she was, exhausted and weighed down by her peasant clothes, which were enough to drown the most skilful swimmer, did not hesitate to endanger her life. She was determined to save me, even though I was the child that she had once offered to God in exchange for her daughter. When she arrived home and lifted me off her shoulders on to the floor, I was still dazed.

For this reason, instead of blaming the incident on my own improvidence, I attributed it to my mother's exertions.

"Don't work any more, mother," I said as she dressed me in dry clothes.

"And who'll feed us if I don't work?" she asked with a sigh.

"I shall, mother, I shall!" I replied with childish bombast.

"And our foster-child?"

"I'll feed her too!"

My mother smiled despite herself to see the imposing stance I adopted while uttering this assurance. Then she cut short our conversation with the words:

"Well, feed yourself first, and then we'll see about that."

It was shortly after this that I was preparing to leave home. Mother naturally took no notice of this promise, but I always remembered that her self-denial had granted me for a second time the life that I owed her. I therefore kept this promise close to my heart, and the more I grew up the more earnestly did I feel obliged to fulfil it.

"Don't cry, mother," I told her as I left. "I'm going off to make lots of money. Don't you worry! From now on I'll feed you and your foster-daughter. But I don't want you to work any more, do you hear?"

I did not know yet that a ten-year-old boy was incapable even of feeding himself, let alone his mother, and I little imagined what fearful adventures were in store for me and how much pain I was to cause my mother by this decision of mine to leave home, by which I hoped to give her some respite. For many years I was unable even to send her a letter, let alone financial help. For many years she stood in wait in the streets, asking travellers whether they had seen me. Sometimes they would tell her I had fallen on bad times in Constantinople and had turned Turk.

"May they swallow their tongues for spreading such rumours!" my mother would retort. "They can't be talking about my boy!"

But after a while she would lock herself up in terror with her icons and pray tearfully to God to enlighten me so that I would return to the faith of my fathers.

Sometimes they would tell her that, having been shipwrecked on the shores of Cyprus, I was now dressed in rags and begging in the streets.

"May they be burned by fire!" she would respond. "They only say that because they're jealous. My boy's probably made his fortune and gone on a pilgrimage to the Holy Sepulchre."

But she would soon be out in the streets scrutinizing passing beggars, and whenever she heard of some shipwrecked voyager she would go and find him in the faint hope of discovering her own son in his person, with the intention of giving him her humble pittance so that I might receive the same treatment from the natives of whatever place I was unfortunate enough to find myself in.

Nonetheless, whenever it came to her adopted daughter, she forgot all this and threatened my brothers that when I returned home I would put them to shame with my munificence and provide a dowry for her daughter, whom I would marry off with pomp and circumstance.

"What? Do you doubt it? My boy promised me, bless him!"

Fortunately, those ill tidings were not true. When, after a long absence, I returned home, I was in a position to fulfil my promise, at least in respect of my mother, who was frugal; but towards her foster-child she did not find me as eager as she had hoped. On the contrary, no sooner had I arrived than I expressed the opinion, much to my mother's surprise, that we should not keep her.

It is true that I was not strictly opposed to my mother's weakness. Her inclination towards girls was in accord with my own feelings and desires. I wanted nothing more than to find, on my return home, a sister whose radiant countenance and compassionate solicitude would banish from my heart the melancholy born of isolation, and expunge from my memory the hardships I had endured in distant lands. In return I would readily have offered to tell her of the wondrous things to be found in foreign countries, my wanderings and my achievements; I would have been eager to buy her anything she wanted, take her to dances and festivals, provide her with a dowry and finally dance at her wedding.

But I had imagined this sister to be beautiful and pleasant, intelligent and well educated, good at handiwork, and with all the virtues that I had found in the girls of those countries in which I had lived until then. And instead of all this, what did I find? Exactly the opposite. Our adoptive sister was small, sickly, ill-formed, ill-tempered and, above all, dull-witted, so dull-witted indeed that she inspired me with aversion from the outset.

"Give Katerinio back," I told my mother one day. "Give her back, if you love me. This time I'm telling you straight. I'll bring you another daughter from Constantinople, a beautiful, intelligent girl who'll adorn our household."

I went on to describe in the liveliest of colours the orphan that I intended to bring her, and how much I would love her. When I raised my eyes to her face, I was surprised to see large teardrops flowing silently down her pale cheeks, while her downcast eyes expressed an indescribable sadness.

"Oh!" she cried desperately. "I thought you would love Katerinio more than the others do, but I was mistaken! They don't want a sister at all, and you want a different one! How can the poor thing help being made as God has made her? If you had an ugly, unintelligent sister, you would throw her out into the street and get another one cleverer and more beautiful."

"No, mother, certainly not," I replied. "She would be your child, as I am. But this girl isn't related to you, she's completely alien to us."

"No," exclaimed my mother, sobbing, "no!" The child is mine! I took her three months old from her mother's corpse and whenever she cried I gave her my breast so as to pacify her. I wrapped her in your swaddling-clothes and put her to sleep in your cradle. She's my child and your sister!"

With these words, which she uttered in a powerful and impressive tone, she raised her head and fixed her gaze upon me, challenging me to reply. But I dared not utter a word. Then she lowered her eyes once more and continued in a weak, mournful voice:

"Well, there's nothing to be done! I would like her to have been better too but, you see, my sin hasn't been put right yet and God made her as she is so as to test my patience and forgive me. I thank you, Lord!"

With that, she placed her right hand on her breast, raised her tearful eyes to heaven, and remained thus for some moments in silence.

"You must have something on your mind," I said with some hesitation. "Don't be angry."

Taking her icy hand, I kissed it to appease her.

"Yes," said she decisively. "I've got something very heavy inside me, my son. Up to now only God and my confessor know it. You're well-read and you sometimes talk like the confessor himself, and better. Go and shut the door, then sit down and le me tell you about it – maybe you'll comfort me a little, maybe you'll be sorry for me and learn to love Katerinio as if she was your sister."

These words, and the way in which she uttered them, put my heart in great turmoil. What had my mother to confide in me separately from my brothers? She had already related to me all the misfortunes she had suffered during my absence, and I knew the whole of her previous life as if it were a fairy-tale. What was it, then, that she had been concealing from us until now? What was it that she had not dared to reveal to anyone save God and her confessor?

When I came back and sat next to her, my knees were trembling with a vague and powerful apprehension. My mother hung her head like a condemned man who stands before his judge with the consciousness of some fearful crime.

"Do you remember our Annio?" she asked after some moments of oppressive silence.

"Of course, mother! How could I forget her? She was our only sister and she passed away before my very eyes."

"Yes," she said with a deep sigh, "but she wasn't my only girl. You are four years younger than Christakis. A year after he was born I had my first daughter.

"It was about the time Fotis Mylonas was about to get married. Your late father delayed their wedding until I came out of confinement so we could marry them together. He wanted to let me come out into society so I could enjoy myself like a married woman, since your grandmother didn't let me enjoy myself when I was a girl.

"We married them in the morning and in the evening the guests came to their house: the violins played, and people ate out in the yard, and the wine-jug was passed around. Your father was in high spirits – he loved to have fun, poor man – and he threw me his handkerchief to invite me to dance. I was thrilled whenever I saw him dance, and I loved dancing too, as young people do. So we danced, and the others danced behind us. But we danced more and better than anyone.

"As midnight drew near, I took your father aside and said, 'Husband, I've got a baby in the cradle and I can't stay any longer. The baby's hungry and I'm heavy with milk. How can I feed her in my best dress and in front of everybody? You stay here if you want to have some more fun; I'll take the baby and go home.'

"'Never mind about that,' he said – God forgive him – and he patted me on the shoulder. 'Come on, dance this one with me, then we'll both go. The wine's begun to go to my head and I'm looking for an excuse to leave.'

"When we'd finished the dance we set off home. The bridegroom sent the musicians to see us half-way down the road, but we still had some way to go because the wedding took place at Karshimahala. The servant went ahead with the lantern and your father carried the baby and held me by the arm.

"'You're tired, I see, wife.'

"'Yes, Michalios, I'm tired.'

"'Come on, keep your strength up a bit more and we'll soon be home. I'll make the beds. I'm sorry now I made you dance so much.'

"'Never mind, husband,' I said, 'I did it to please you. Tomorrow I'll be able to rest.'

"And so we got home. I swaddled the baby and fed her, and he made the beds. Christakis was still sleeping with Venetia, and I let her look after him. Soon we went to bed too. Then, in my sleep, I fancied the baby started crying. Poor thing, I said, she didn't eat enough today. I leaned over her cradle to feed her, but I was tired and couldn't stand up, so I lifted her out and laid her down next to me in bed and gave her the breast. Then I fell asleep again.

"I don't know how long it was till morning, but when I sensed dawn breaking I said to myself, 'I'll put the baby back.'

"But when I went to pick her up, what did I see? The baby wasn't moving!

"I woke your father; we undressed her, tried to warm her up, rubbed her little nose, but nothing happened! She was dead!

"'You've smothered the baby, wife!' said your father, and burst into tears. Then I began to sob and wail. But your father put his hand over my mouth and said, 'Shush! What are you yelling like that for, you great idiot?' That's what he said, God forgive him. We'd been married three years and he'd never said a harsh word to me till that moment. 'What are you yelling like that for, eh? Do you want to wake the whole neighbourhood so people will say you got drunk and smothered your baby?'

"He was right – may he rest in peace – because if people had found out, I would have had to dig a hole in the ground and disappear into it from shame.

"But there we are. A sin's a sin. When we buried the baby and came back from the church, that was when my great lamenting began. I didn't weep secretly any longer. 'You're young and you'll have other children,' people told me. But time passed and God didn't grant us anything. 'There,' I said to myself. 'God's punishing me because I wasn't capable of protecting the baby He gave me!' I felt ashamed in front of other people, and I was afraid of your father. The whole of the first year he consoled me and pretended not to be sad so as to encourage me. But later on he began to be silent and pensive.

"Three years went by without my enjoying a single bite of food. But exactly three years later you were born.

"When you were born I was very relieved, but I still wasn't able to calm down. Your father wanted you to be a girl, and one day he told me so.

"'This baby's all very welcome, Despinio, but I wanted it to be a girl.'

"When your grandmother went to the Holy Sepulchre, I sent twelve shirts and three gold coins so she would get me an absolution. And, lo and behold, the very month that your grandmother got back from Jerusalem with the absolution, I went into labour with Annio.

"Every so often I would call the midwife. 'Come on, let's see, is it a girl?' 'Yes, daughter,' she would say, 'a girl. Can't

you see? You're too big for your clothes.' How happy I was
to hear it!

"When the baby was born and it turned out to be a girl,
I found comfort at last. We called her Annio, the same as
the other poor baby, so it wouldn't seem there was anyone
missing from our household. 'Thank you, Lord,' I used to
say day and night. 'Thank you, Lord, for removing my
shame and expunging my sin, unworthy as I am!'

"So we pampered Annio, and you almost died of jeal-
ousy. Your father used to call you his 'poor wronged child',
because I weaned you early, and he sometimes scolded me
for neglecting you. I was terribly distressed to see you pining away but, you see, I couldn't let go of Annio! I was
afraid that something might happen to her at any moment,
and your late father, no matter how much he scolded me,
wanted her to be cosseted!

"But the more the poor mite was coddled, the less
healthy she became. It was as if God had regretted giving
her to us. The rest of you were rosy-cheeked and lively and
sprightly, whereas she was quiet and indolent and sickly.
Whenever I saw her so pale I recalled the dead baby, and I
was obsessed with the idea that I had caused her death.
Then one day the second one died too!

"Anyone who hasn't gone through the same experience,
my son, doesn't know what a bitter cup that was. There was
no hope of my having another girl because your father had
died. If I hadn't found a parent to give me his daughter I
would have taken to the hills.

"It's true she didn't turn out to be good-natured, but as
long as I cared for her and fondled her I thought of her as
my own; I forgot the one I lost and my conscience was easy.

As the saying goes, another's child is a trial. But for me this trial was a comfort and a relief because the more I'm tormented and exasperated, the less God will punish me for the child I smothered. So if you want my blessing, don't ask me to get rid of Katerinio and get a good-natured, co-operative child."

"No, no, mother," I cried, unable to restrain myself. "I ask nothing. After what you've told me I beg your forgiveness for my callousness. I promise to love Katerinio as my own sister and never say anything nasty to her again."

"May Christ and the Virgin Mary bless you," said mother, breathing a sigh of relief. "You see, my heart bled for the poor orphan, and I don't want anyone to speak ill of her. Whether it's the fault of God or fate that she's so spiteful and incompetent, she's my responsibility all the same."

This revelation made a profound impression on me. Now that my eyes had been opened, I understood many of my mother's actions which had seemed to me to be the consequence of superstition or sheer obsession. That fearful accident had affected my mother's whole existence all the more because she was so artless, virtuous and pious. The consciousness of sin, the moral need for an expiation that could never be achieved – what a frightful and relentless Hell this was! For twenty-eight years now the poor woman had been tormented without being able to salve her conscience, either in good fortune or in adversity.

As soon as I learned her sorry story, I focused all my attention on ways of lightening her heart by pointing out to her on the one hand the unpremeditated and unintentional nature of her sin, and on the other the supreme compassion of God, His justice, which does not repay like with like, but judges us according to our thoughts and our intentions. For a time I believed my efforts were not entirely fruitless. Nevertheless, when, after a renewed absence of two years, my mother came to see me in Constantinople, I judged it appropriate to do something more impressive on her behalf.

I was then staying at the most distinguished house in Constantinople, where I had occasion to become acquainted with Patriarch Joachim II. One day, while we were walking together in the abundant shade of the garden, I expounded the story to him and appealed to him for assistance. His supreme office and the special authority with which his every religious pronouncement was invested would undoubtedly convince my mother that her sin had been forgiven. The venerable old man, praising my zeal in religious matters, promised me his eager co-operation.

Thus it was that I took my mother to the Patriarchate in order to confess to His Holiness. The confession lasted a long time, and from the Patriarch's words and gestures I concluded that he needed to exert the full force of his unadorned and easily comprehensible rhetoric in order to achieve the desired result.

My joy was ineffable. My mother bade farewell to the elderly Patriarch with sincere gratitude and left the Patriarchate looking as pleased and relieved as if a great millstone had been lifted from her heart. When we arrived at her lodgings, she pulled out from the front of her dress a cross which His Holiness had given her. She kissed it and began to scrutinize it, sinking gradually deeper in thought.

"That Patriarch's a good man," I said, "don't you think? Now at last I believe you've found comfort."

My mother made no reply.

"Haven't you anything to say, mother?" I asked her hesitantly.

"What can I say, my son?" she replied pensively. "The Patriarch's a wise and holy man. He knows all the intentions of God and he forgives everyone's sins. But how can I put it? He's a monk. He's never had children, and he can't know what it means to kill your own child!"

Her eyes filled with tears, and I remained silent.

Who was my brother's murderer?

"I'm really going to enjoy my food today at last!" said my mother, seated between me and my brother at the frugal table that the valet had set in our room.

"Actions speak louder than words, mother," my brother teased her, since for some time he had heard this good intention expressed but had never seen it carried out.

Mother, accustomed to such remarks from her youngest son, paid no attention to his words. Instead she turned towards the door behind her to make sure it was closed, and said:

"And don't let that wagtail come here again. I've had enough of his bobbing up and down."

The "wagtail" was the French valet at the hotel on the Bosporus where my mother had come to meet me on my arrival from the West. The clean-shaven Frenchman's tail coat, so unfamiliar to the countrywoman's eyes, together with his continual bowing and scraping, inspired an incomprehensible antipathy in her from the outset. The worst thing was that in his desire to gain her favour the unfortunate valet increased his bobbing up and down, bowing in such an apish fashion that my mother's exasperation with him reached a peak even during those first days, and she had dubbed him "wagtail" because, she said, he had a womanly (that is, clean-shaven) face and couldn't stand on his pins without bowing his head and wagging his tail.

After some further derisory remarks about the general bearing and attire of the unfortunate Louis, my mother almost imperceptibly interrupted her meal and, fixing her gaze on the window, gradually sank into thought, as was her wont. The Bosporus was flowing delightfully beneath us; numerous fragile-looking craft were gliding through the azure waters in opposite directions, like swallows flying with matchless speed. My mother stared at them blankly, then after a long silence said with a sigh:

"See how the years pass and things turn out unexpectedly! My son won't return, I used to say; he won't come back before I die, and my eyes will stay open from their longing to see him. All day long I used to keep watch on the streets and ask passers-by, and when it got dark I used to leave the door open till midnight. 'Don't shut it yet, Michailo, my son may come yet and I don't want him to arrive and find my door closed. It's bad enough his being all alone in a far-off land for so many years, without his coming to his village and thinking he's got no one in the world to wait for him to arrive.' When I went to bed, I used to see you in my sleep, I fancied I could hear your voice, and I used to get up and open the door and ask: 'Have you come, my son?' But it was the wind whispering in the street.

"And so it would go on, day and night. Eight whole years went by, and I never enjoyed a single bite of food. Because, I said to myself, my son won't come back before I die, and my eyes will stay open! Now, see! Now that you're near me, now that I see you, it seems like yesterday that you left, and it's as though all the griefs and fears I've gone through never happened!"

At this she mechanically broke off a piece of bread, as if she wished to continue her meal; but without putting it in her mouth, she stared out of the window again, saw the continuous flow of the Bosporus and the toing and froing of the boats, and sighing from the depths of her heart, repeated slowly and mournfully:

"How the years pass and things turn out unexpectedly! I was expecting trouble from one quarter, and it came from the one where I was least expecting it! You went to the ends of the earth, my son, and returned safe and sound, while our Christakis went on a five-hour journey and never came back! Only the dead don't return!

"It was the eve of Epiphany – you know how I feel on such holy-days. I remembered your late father, and I recalled that one Epiphany-eve, when you saw the local children holding rowan branches and "rowaning" people in the streets, you grabbed a broom and started hitting your father on the back and rowaning him: 'Rowan, rowan! Sturdy body, sturdy loins, health and strength for years to come!' You knew the words, small as you were. Your poor father was thrilled and took you in his arms and kissed you: 'Now you grow into a big boy, bless you!' He gave you a penny and wagged his finger at me and said, 'Wife, that boy'll go far!' He wasn't to know he would leave you an orphan three months later! And he wasn't to know Epiphany eve would come and go and you would be suffering far away and I would be left crying all alone!

"So it was on that Epiphany eve. Michailos, who knew my mind, went up the hill early in the morning and brought back a rowan-bough, a big bough covered with tight green buds. 'Tonight we'll tell our fortunes, mother, with these rowan-twigs.' When Christakis came home, we sat by the hearth and divided the fire into two, and Michailos began putting the rowan-twigs in the middle, on the red-hot slab, so we could tell our fortunes. First of all he said your name and cut off a rowan-twig and put it on. As soon as he'd put it on, it burst and jumped out of the hearth. 'Bless you, Michailo!' I said. 'You've gladdened my heart tonight. As long as our Yorgis is healthy, we're all well!' Then he said my name. Well, I did all right too, I suppose. Then he said Christakis' name, and see! the rowan-shoot stayed quietly on the slab where he'd put it, without moving, till it went black and put out smoke and turned a little and burned away! Lord, child!' I said to him, 'you didn't put a good twig on!' I took the branch from his hand and chose the best shoot; I made a fresh place in the fire and put it there. It smoked a little, went black, stretched out and stayed where it was! Then Christakis laughed loudly and picked up a brand and stirred the embers.

"'Mother,' he said, 'I'm a tough man, you know. I don't just jump out when it gets a bit hot like you two. If you want to know my fortune, look here!'

"He took the branch from my hand and put it in the fire. The twigs caught fire and began bursting and jumping about.

"Now you can say what you like: rowan-twigs are rowan-twigs, I know, and it's true that people tell fortunes as a matter of custom rather than to find out the truth. But when I remember that hollow popping sound and those distant gunshots we began to hear around the villages a few days later, my heart is troubled and I can't find rest. It was clear as day, but we took no notice; we took it lightly and just laughed.

"While we were laughing, the door opened and in came Charalambis, Mitakos' son. You remember him – he was the same age as Christakis and very like him in build. When he was a child he often used to come to our house, but when he grew up and got into bad ways I couldn't bear the sight of him, because often, when he was up to no good, he used to be mistaken for Christakis. They were so alike, and because they were in the same line of business they even wore the same clothes. So one day I gave him a good dressing down and after that he never set foot inside our front door. But that evening he came.

"'Good evening, ma'am! I hope you're well.'

"'Hello, Lambis. If you've brought me a letter, sit down and have a drink.'

"'No, ma'am, I've given up the post. In fact, I've come to tell Christakis not to let anyone but him take the job.'

"At this, I began to get worried.

"'Why not, Lambis?'

"'Because the postman's job's a good one, ma'am, a good job!'

"'If it's such a good job, then why don't you keep it yourself?'

"You'd think someone had stabbed him: his expression changed and he began mincing his words.

"'Well, ma'am, I've been fetching the post from the railway for two years and I've made plenty of money. Let my friends have a go now.'

"'Listen here, Lambis,' I said. 'Even if you have made

money, as they say, we don't need that sort of money, I tell you! Anyway, you can't get away with that kind of trickery any more, and the man who fetches the post can't grow rich on the meagre savings sent by some orphaned emigrant to pay for a memorial service for his father. As for that other skill that made you rich, Lambis, God will be your judge. My son's an honest Christian and he knows how to earn his living by the sweat of his brow.'

"I spoke to him like that because I knew he was a thief. And as I spoke, he went all of a tremble, his lips turned ashen and his eyes grew fierce as if he was having a fit. Oh Lord! Three times he opened his mouth to speak and each time I heard his teeth chattering, but he didn't utter a sound! His face was deathly pale and all twisted up, and I could see utter terror in his frightened eyes as they stole furtive glances at his clothes and his right hand, even between his fingers! It was as if he was smeared with something and was afraid we'd see it. Then, after this horrific struggle, he spoke – Lord! it was like the voice of someone choking:

"'Don't listen to what people say, ma'am. I'm a good man!'

"And with that he hid his face in his hands and went out without saying goodnight.

"'Do you see, mother?' said Christakis. 'You didn't believe me when I told you. He's killed someone and the blood's turned against him. Everyone says so, only you don't believe it. If you say you've found out he's done something – even if it's just to try him out – he thinks you're talking about the murder. He thinks the blood has appeared on his hands to betray him.'

"'Since you didn't see it with your own eyes, it's not for you to malign him. Every lamb is hanged by its own foot. If it's true, God will be his judge, so he'll get his just deserts. But do me the favour of not getting involved in the post – he wouldn't give it up without good reason.'

"'Can't you understand what I'm saying, mother?' he said. 'The blood has turned against him. The blood he shed on the road haunts him and doesn't let him pass. The other day he had to turn back half-way and leave the post behind. He saw someone lying in wait for him, do you hear – it must have been the blood. They say that if anyone kills a man and doesn't think to lick the blood off the knife, the blood will haunt him and choke him one day, or it'll torment him till he confesses and they hang him.'

"'For my sake, my son, don't upset me any more. And, for God's sake, don't stir these things up, because if the authorities hear about it you'll be in trouble. Let the post and the postman go hang, and mind your own business like a good lad.'

"But the poor boy – you know how he was – could never sit still for a moment. I had him learn a trade and I opened a workshop for him so he would take his father's place, but he preferred to wander about the streets!

"'It's five hours' walk from here to Lüleburgaz,' he said. 'I'm only going to go there and back once a fortnight – why should I let someone else benefit from it?'

"'No, I beg you! I won't let you fetch the post! Promise me you won't do it, or you'll ruin my peace of mind!'

"'Oh, very well!' he said. 'I won't do it. But you just go for two months without a letter and see if you don't regret it!'

"That touched a sensitive spot. Your letters used not to

come regularly because they would be opened on the way. They weren't content to take things out of the envelopes, but then they were ashamed to bring them opened, and so I used to go without any news from you, and I used to sit and cry. But I didn't say anything to him – I'd suffered so long that I could go on suffering a bit more.

"When post-day came, I saw him come in with the official bag over one shoulder and the gun over the other.

"'Now, mother,' he said, 'you won't give the tip to some stranger. You'll give it to me when I bring you bring you Yorgis' letter tomorrow. All right?'

"About twelve days had passed since the evening when I'd tried to persuade him not to go. As usual, the Epiphany-eve fortune-telling had been forgotten. But I hadn't forgotten Mitakos' son, so I began chiding him for being reckless. But he wouldn't listen! He'd taken the obligation upon himself. He'd promised the village elders and the provincial governor.

"When I realized I was wasting my breath, I gave him my letter to you. 'Be sure not to lose Yorgis' letter, son!' I said. I can see him now! He took off his fez, kissed my hand and went off. Who could have known we should have stopped him?

"Next day the new bishop was to come. The church officials and the elders had gone to the station first thing; the teachers and schoolchildren were lined up, and the priests and the rest of the villagers went about an hour's journey up the road to welcome him. Michailos went with them. The village was practically empty. The time for the post came, but I wasn't worried about Christakis: he would certainly come with the bishop's retinue. The weather was fine, and I kept watch out of the window. When I saw the people in the distance coming back, I straightened my scarf and went out of the village to kiss the bishop's hand. The church banners and the golden disc with the seraphs on it flashed in the sun from a long way off, and behind them gleamed the crosses and the priests' chasubles. Behind them, to one side, I could make out a white horse with gold trappings that had been taken to fetch the bishop, but as it got nearer there was no bishop to be seen. I was puzzled and anxious, so I hurried out to take a closer look.

"'Go back, ma'am!' shouted one of the boys who were running at the front of the procession in their festive clothes. 'Go back! The army's coming! They've cut the railway line and taken the bishop!'

"I felt my blood run cold. There had been talk of war, but the Russians were a long way off in the Balkans, we were told, or even further away. And now they'd suddenly cut the railway line. Something's bound to happen to the boy, I said to myself. I was so scared I couldn't move. Then the crowd arrived terrified and in a hurry. The Cross appeared with the banners, the priest appeared with the censer, and four people appeared with a corpse on their shoulders, with Michailos beside them all dishevelled and in floods of tears. Oh, my son, my son! Who could have known he should have been prevented from going?"

At this point her trembling voice was drowned by her weeping and sobbing.

It was the first time that day. Knowing my poor mother's nature, I did not interrupt her, nor did I let my brother do so. Grief was flooding over her loving heart, and if she did not let it overflow once or twice or thrice a day, she could not find relief. The frightful trauma had struck our already grief-stricken household three years and more before, but my recent arrival (since I had not witnessed the fearful drama from close at hand) re-opened the unfortunate woman's scarcely healed wounds. My presence made us feel my brother's loss all the more since, as my mother rightly put it, our joy could never be complete. Few as my loved ones were, I found them ever fewer and fewer. I could not kiss my poor brother, nor could he ever again rejoice at the return of the brother who was so long awaited. So the un-happy woman wept as she told that sorrowful tale, as if it had happened the previous day.

When the floods of tears had lightened her grieving heart a little, she appeared to forget her sorrow. But in re-ality her grief at our dear brother's murder had given way to implacable fury against his murderer.

"Sometimes," my brother told me in private, "I've thought she was beginning to forget Christakis, but I've never seen her forget his murderer."

In the meantime she had not stopped badgering both the bishop and the governor to make them find her son's murderer. At first it was thought he had been killed by ac-cident during the attack on Lüleburgaz station, but this was soon shown to have been impossible. Those who had come to collect the prelate found that the station had been abandoned by the local authorities two days previously – since when all communications with Constantinople had been severed – and the Russians had captured the village without a fight no earlier than the middle of the previous night. The same people discovered my poor brother during their disorderly return, next to the bridge along the highway at a considerable distance from the village, and he had died well before the arrival of the Russians. He had not, then, been killed accidentally, nor in a military engagement; nor could he have been deliberately killed by soldiers or robbers, since the former would not have left the body undespoiled, and the latter would not have left his post-bag intact. All official enquiries led to the palpable conclusion that he had been killed in an ambush, but not for the purposes of robbery. It was for this reason that my mother insisted that the murderer should be found and punished. The way in which the disreputable former postman had persuaded the unsuspecting youth to succeed him in his dangerous task provided her enquiries with a vital clue.

"It can't be otherwise," she said. "The murderer must have been in a fury with him, and he must have known it. Otherwise he couldn't have lain in wait for Christakis the very first day he took on the post. So he's bound to be someone from the village or thereabouts. When the man who'd had the job before was taken off to prison, I thought God had passed his judgement. But two days later he was let out because they found he'd been in the village when the murder happened. Who knows? Maybe they gave false evidence... But now you've come, my son, don't let your brother go unavenged. Don't look at me like that in silence! If I didn't have son I'd cut off my hair, put on men's clothes and track down the murderer, with my rifle over my shoulder, till I avenged the murder. You see, my son, poor Christakis can't find rest, he tosses about in his grave very time he feels his murderer treading the earth. He feels him, my son – even if he's at the other end of the world, he feels him as if he's trampling on his heart! So vengeance must be taken! Vengeance!"

Anyone who had not known this loving mother before her son's death would certainly have taken her to be a woman of a harsh and cruel nature, for even I could hardly detect in her that infinite kind-heartedness which made her show such mercy and compassion towards brute nature that she could not bear to see even a chicken slaughtered. By "vengeance" she really meant justice, but she could not conceive of this justice being meted out by the impassive hand of the law alone, without her personal satisfaction.

"Let me see him hang," she said, "so I can pull the rope – then let me die!"

How frightfully desirable did vengeance seem to the loving nature of that simple untutored woman! The cold arguments of erudition, with which I sometimes sought to calm the impulses of her fervent heart, evaporated before they could reach their goal, like tiny drops of water falling in an intensely burning furnace. After a lengthy sermon on the place of the individual in relation to the laws of the state, I promised her that I would move heaven and earth to bring the culprit to justice. Then, with ferocious delight, she said:

"Yes! Let me see him hang so I can pull the rope – then let me die!"

Suddenly there was a knock at the door and, with obvious displeasure, she saw the clean-shaven face of the valet reverentially peeping in.

"What is it, Louis?" I asked him as he came in.

"It's a Turkish woman," he replied, bowing to my scowling mother; "a Turkish woman come to visit you."

"Come to visit us? But that's impossible! You must be mistaken, Louis. Please go, we don't know any Turkish women."

But even as I was dismissing him for my mother's sake, I heard a commotion and the sound of quarrelling in the corridor. Louis bowed once more as low as possible in order to convince me that the visit was indeed intended for us. Suddenly the door burst open with a bang, knocking him headlong to the floor, and an elderly Turkish lady, scarcely covered by her veil, flung herself at my mother's feet amid sobs and tears. It seems that the valets outside had been preventing her from entering, and in desperation she had forced open the door. The flabbergasted Louis had sufficiently recovered his composure to kick out the tall, white-turbaned *softa*[1] who was following her, when my brother, on seeing the young man, intervened to reprimand the valet and admit the pale, lean Turk with such joy as if he were his closest friend.

"It's our Kamil," he told me rather pompously, "and this is his mother!"

My mother, freeing herself with some difficulty from the Turkish lady's embrace, looked up with strange affection at the pleasant features of the *softa* and said:

"Is it you, Kamil, my son? How are you? Are you well? I didn't recognize you in that costume!"

The Turk bent down and with tears in his eyes kissed the hem of her dress.

"May God bring you blessings, *Validé*!" he said.[2] "I pray

---

1. Muslim theological student.
2. *Validé*: Mother (Ottoman honorific title).

to Him day and night to take years off my life and add them to yours."

My mother looked exceedingly gratified, while Michailos seemed beside himself with joy, lavishing countless attentions on the tall, gaunt man in the green cassock and on the latter's mother. Louis and I alone stood in baffled silence. At length I took my brother aside.

"Come on, stop laughing," I said, "and tell me what's going on here. Who *are* these people?"

"I'll tell you," replied my brother, laughing even more. "I'll tell you. Louis, go and fetch two coffees quickly, but see you don't make them like your Frenchie dishwater! Turkish-style, and no sugar, do you hear?"

With that, he led me into the adjoining room.

"He's a Turk who mother looked after at home for seven months when he was ill, and that's his mother who's come to say thank-you to her," said my brother, laughing again, to my great surprise.

"A Turk who mother looked after for seven months? Since when has mother been a nurse to Turks?" I asked, frowning with indignation.

I must point out that Michailos was in the habit of jesting at our mother's whims, all the more gladly in that he willingly and uncomplainingly paid for them out of his own purse. Nothing amused him more than to mimic our mother in the grip of one of her whims, exaggerating her manner to uniquely comic effect. Mother used to laugh too when she heard him, and her forbearance encouraged this bad habit of his to become even more deeply rooted. Therefore, when he saw my indignation at what I heard, he said:

"Now listen here! If you mean to stand there with a long face, I'm not telling you anything. You'll spoil my story. Let's leave it till another day so you can laugh your head off and mother can laugh a bit too, because she hasn't had a good laugh for days, poor thing!"

"Come now," I said. "Mother seems pleased with the visit and she's completely occupied with those Turks of hers, whom I can't abide. Tell me the story while they're drinking their coffee and leaving us in peace."

"Listen, then," he said. "You know how worried mother used to be when you were away. Well, she wasn't content to be worried herself, but she used to get everyone else worried too. If anyone came by, she would stop him in the street; if anyone arrived in the village, she would go and ask him if he'd seen you or heard about you. You know her! Early one morning we were gathering melons in the field when suddenly she sees a traveller going by. Instead of letting him go about his business, she runs over to the fence.

"'Good morning, uncle.'

"'Greetings, ma'am.'

"'Are you coming from Europe?'

"'No, ma'am, from my village. Where's this Europe anyway?'

"'Well, I don't rightly know, but it's where my son is. Haven't you heard tell of my son?'

"'No, ma'am. What's his name?'

"'Well, I don't quite know. His godfather baptized him Yorgis and his father was Michalios the pedlar – my husband. But, you see, he's gone up in the world and taken one of those highfalutin names, and now when I see it in the papers I don't know if it's my son or some Frenchie!'"

"The story, Michailo! The story of the Turk!" I interrupted him impatiently.

"Hold on!" he said. "The story comes after the conversation. So after this, mother cuts the best and biggest melon.

"'Would you like a melon from our garden, uncle?'

"'No thanks, ma'am, I've got nowhere to put it.'

"'Never mind, uncle, I'll cut it up so you can eat it.'

"'No thanks, ma'am, I've got bellyache.'

"'Come on, do me a favour. You see, I've got a son in a strange land and I miss him so much. I can't send it to him, so at least you can eat it because you're a stranger. Then perhaps someone else will give *him* some.'

"The man lost his patience.

"'Look here, my good woman! It's not my fault that you son's in a strange land, and I'm certainly not going to put that rubbish in my belly before breakfast. D'you think I'm tired of life? If you really want to put your melon to good use, why don't you send it to old Mourtos' inn? Somewhere round there there's a stranger who's been fighting for his life for three weeks with a fever. You take my word for it, as soon as he tastes that rubbish he'll be shot of his fever and his fever'll be shot of him!"

"Really now," I interrupted him, "have you finished with the trivial details? Get down to the story!"

"Just a moment!" he replied in a bantering tone. "We're not in Europe where they sell meat without the bones! I'm telling you the story as it happened. If you don't like it, you can lump it. Let's go and see the *hanum*!

"You should have been there," he continued, "to see mother when she heard it that. 'Lord in Heaven – my son!'

The melon dropped from her hands and was smashed to pulp. She straightened her scarf and started down the road – or rather, straight across the sown and unsown fields, so as to get there as soon as possible. I knew her ways, so I let her go. But when she had gone some way and saw I hadn't moved, she turned round and shouted angrily:

"What are you standing there gaping for, you idiot? Are you waiting for me to tell you to budge?'

"There was nothing to do but follow her: she was capable of chucking a clod of earth at my head. So I left my work and set off behind her. But how could I keep up with her? Brambles, ditches, fences – she saw nothing except the roof of old Mourtos' house standing out red amid the crops.

"When she got near, her knees began to shake and she sat down on a stone.

"'Lord in Heaven, son, why didn't you tell me there was someone sick here?'

"'Why should I have told you? You're not a doctor, are you? Even father Dimos didn't go and see him when he heard about him. He's a Turk, he said, and Turks don't pay for extreme unction.'

"'A Turk, did you say?' she cried, her face resuming its normal features. 'Well, if it's a Turk, thank God! I was afraid it might be our Yorgis!'

"'Pity I didn't tell you before, mother, so you wouldn't have ruined everybody's fields and riddled my feet with thorns. You were in such a hurry, you made me set off barefoot.'

"Meanwhile she started off again towards Mourtos' inn. I'd begun following and was just about to jump over a ditch when I heard someone groaning. I turned round, and what did I see? A Turk on the ground with a pale face and red eyes. Now, however readily I laugh normally, I've never laughed at a sick man. But on this occasion I couldn't contain myself. You can't imagine what was going on. On one side there was a brier and on the other a wild artichoke, and the Turk was thrashing about between them and babbling away. First he would turn to the brier, salute it, then start paying court to it and giving it the glad eye. Then he would turn on the artichoke, grind his teeth, look daggers at it, abuse it and raise his hand as if to cut off its head! The combination of his grand words and his ineffectual actions was enough to make you die laughing. But when mother came and saw me she got into such a temper! Lord save you from such a temper!

"'What are you standing there cackling for? There's a man at death's door and all you can do is laugh! Catch hold of him and lift him onto your back!'

"'Come on now, he's half as tall again as I am. How do you expect me to lift him onto my back?'

"'Pick him up, I tell you, or else!'

"There was nothing to do but obey her. So I picked up the huge Turk, loaded him on my back and we set off. Old Mourtos was sunning his belly outside his inn door. When he saw us he laughed deep down in his throat and shouted:

"'Hey, why don't you try picking up that dead donkey over there so you can at least sell its hooves, instead of thrashing about like that just so as to carry the plague home with you?'

"I didn't reply because, as you can imagine, I didn't have any breath to spare for jokes. But mother – you know mother! She really laid into him for being so callous.

"When we got him home, we laid him on Christakis' bed. Poor Christakis was going around the neighbouring villages with his wares on horseback in those days. It was before he opened his shop. When he heard we had a sick man in the house, he went and put up at our aunt's house at Kryoneró. Mother was always telling him off for his disorderly behaviour and he was looking for an excuse to stay out of the house. So he never set foot over our threshold in all those seven months that we had the sick man in the house. In the end mother was forced to send him to Constantinople before he was completely cured."

"How did he fetch up at the village," I enquired. "And how did he come to fall ill?"

"Hm!" said my brother, scratching his head. "I only know bits and pieces of the story. Even though I wanted to ask him, mother never let me.

"'We're all human,' she said, 'and illnesses are sent to human beings. Woe betide anyone who hasn't got someone to look after him! Who knows if our Yorgis isn't ill in a strange land at this very moment, with none of his nearest and dearest beside him? So don't sit there interrogating the poor fellow – cure him first!'

"Poor Kamil's a good chap, a very good chap," my brother went on, "and many times he volunteered to tell me how he fell ill. But whenever he tried to do so, he would start shaking with fever."

At that point we were interrupted by my mother, who came in with her visitors. The short and rather plump Turkish lady had arranged her immaculate white yashmak and had adjusted her long black coat, below whose skirts one could just make out her pointed yellow babouches. But what made the deepest impression on me now was the pale, sad face of Kamil, whose features looked so gentle and sweet that they won my affection as if by storm. This did not escape my mother, who knew my dislike for Turks. Thus, looking at him affectionately as she introduced him to me, she said:

"Poor Kamil, he's such a good boy. He eats Christian funeral cakes and drinks holy water and kisses the priest's hand – anything to get cured."

His mother's eyes filled with tears. No sooner had I addressed a couple of words to them in their language than they began showering me with blessings and good wishes, praises and compliments, with the exaggeration characteristic of Turkish etiquette. But my mother abruptly interrupted their cascades of oratory.

"Sit down now," she said, "and let's see what to do. The *hanum* has a son in the police who's one of the leading investigating magistrates. I've told her about the calamity that happened to us and she's going to get him to find the murderer! Poor thing, you don't know how kind she is! What a shame I didn't know, else I'd have come to Constantinople before. I'd have hanged the culprit three times by now and my mind would have been easy on that score at least!"

The Turkish woman understood a little of what my mother was saying.

"Yes," she said, "and my son the Effendi and your servant Kamil and I, your slave, won't abandon your case, even if we have to go to the Sultan's door. Up to now they must have kept it under the carpet, and that's why the murderer hasn't been caught. My son the Effendi's an examining magistrate, and even if the ground's opened up and swallowed the criminal, he'll still find him."

"And," continued Kamil in his pleasant tones, "there won't be a penny to pay! The Effendi my brother will arrange everything with a stroke of the pen. And, God willing, I'll go off into the provinces too to help the investigation. When my *Validé's* son was killed, it was as if the Effendi my brother was killed. Vengeance must be taken!"

The eagerness of them both caused indescribable pleasure not only to my mother but also to my brother and even myself, as I realized how that beneficence towards people of another faith had not been in vain. We discussed the matter for some time and, whereas I had held out no hope of discovering the murderer in view of the time that had elapsed and the disasters that had befallen our region immediately after the killing as a result of the war, I soon became convinced that justice might possibly be done to our dead brother. It was therefore natural that I now began to show more consideration towards the only people who were capable of assisting me in the fulfilment of this duty of ours. As soon as the old Turkish lady observed my disposition, she said:

"And now, my Sultan, hand the keys back to the hotelier: from now on you are my guests."

This was completely unexpected. The Turks, especially in the large towns, not only avoid living under the same roof with Christians, but do not even tolerate them in the same neighbourhood. What did this mean, then? Was it just one of her many servile compliments? But no, the old lady did not mean it as a formality.

"You're an educated man," she told me, "and you know

God's law. Even if I had just one inch of space in the world and I knew that this lady, who looked after my poor orphan for seven months on her own son's bed, was here as a stranger and I didn't give her my pillow to rest her feet on, then wouldn't God close the door of His mercy on my prayer? Wouldn't He remove his blessing from the works of my hands? Wouldn't he turn away His face from my sacrifice? Come, my dear, don't cause me to be damned!"

"Don't be offended," interposed Kamil, kissing the hem of my coat, "that we didn't come and fetch you earlier. Ever since we found out two days ago that you were in town we've been trying to find you. We went through all the caravanserais and sifted through the whole city. But we're simple people and not very bright. It stands to reason that a gentleman like yourself would go about in European style and would be staying in a hotel. Now we've found you, you can't refuse. Isn't that so, my Sultana?" he added, addressing my mother. "That infidel Louis won't put you out of humour again. For your sake I'll forgive him the kick he gave me, but we won't stay here any longer. Isn't that so?"

"That's right," said my mother. "We won't stay, as long as Yorgis agrees. Fancy that wagtail hitting my son, my Kamil!"

"I realized then that, while my brother was telling me Kamil's story, the other three had hatched a plot against the hotelier and Louis. The old Turkish lady launched into a typically oriental vow: "Seven times shall I sit outside your dwellings; seven times a day shall I kiss your threshold; seven times an hour…", etc. – while seven times I lost my patience. Nevertheless, this invitation seemed to me to favour our cause, so I let my mother do as she saw fit.

Half an hour had scarcely passed before the Turkish

lady and her son were leaving in veritable triumph, taking my mother and brother with them as if they were the most highly prized booty. Since neither my business nor my inclinations permitted me to change lodgings, I forbore to accept the offer of their hospitality. I did, however, promise that as soon as I had completed my initial approaches to the competent authorities regarding the search for my brother's murderer I would pay them a long visit each day at their home.

The task did not take me long for, where the law resides only in the goodwill of the various authorities, the simplest case may drag on interminably and the most complex may be completed in an instant. Our own case could not be expected to finish in a flash, but even in the first few days of my dealings with the police ministry, many arrests were ordered in our region, while the investigating magistrate, the son of our friend the Turkish lady, full of eagerness and devotion, set out from the capital accompanied by my brother and equipped with the authority to question those arrested and pursue other suspects. We did not allow the impatient Kamil to go with them, partly because of his precarious health and partly because we did not want the two women to remain alone.

"Now we've poured water into the channel," my mother said to me after a few days, "come and spend the day with us, my son. We're at home all day now that we've finished our sightseeing. Kamil and the *hanum* have taken us everywhere! First we went to see Agia Sophia,[3] then they

---

3. The greatest church in Constantinople, built in the sixth century; in Vizyenos' time it was used as a mosque.

took me to pay my respects at Constantine's tomb at Mefa Meydan.[4] You should go there too, my son! On one side they've buried the negro who killed him, all covered in silks and rugs, and on the other there's the poor emperor with nothing but a little icon-lamp on his tomb. We went to a mosque and saw the chain in an old tree where the Hand of Justice used to hang. We went to Balikli and saw the fish that came alive in the frying-pan when Constantinople was captured. And up on the gate that the conquerors came through we saw the letters written by the angel that day about Constantinople: 'From bad to worse'. I couldn't read them, though, because I'm uneducated. But I didn't need to because we can see every day how Constantinople's going. We've been everywhere and seen everything, but now we've finished I've started getting upset again. So come and see me every day, there's a good boy, and tell me all about how our case is going."

The Turkish widow's house is situated in Divan Yolu, that now broad but no longer picturesque street not far from the Byzantine hippodrome. It is clearly the old property of a once prosperous family. For while the frontages of the neighbouring houses appear to have been mercilessly sliced off to allow the street to be widened, the Turkish lady's house is distinguished by a forecourt, which is very narrow today and certainly possesses but a fraction of its former spaciousness but which allows those sitting on the balcony to look over the low wall at what is happening in the street. Behind the house there is a charming little garden

---

4. Constantine XII, the last emperor of Byzantium, killed during the capture of Constantinople by the Turks in 1453.

with high ivy-clad walls and a small kiosk on one side. It is these walls that saved the greater part of the house from the huge fire that reduced the whole quarter behind the street to ashes. Part of the wall on the opposite side from the kiosk, having collapsed, it seems, during the fire, was rebuilt in a makeshift manner, allowing a small gate to be inserted, whereby a new and more direct access to the house was gained by anyone approaching it through the immense area of ruins from the police ministry. Nevertheless, this spaciousness in one direction was vitiated by the loss suffered in the fire by the breadth of the house. Financial difficulties had not allowed the damaged side to be repaired, and timbers that had been roughly nailed together left the rooms on that side exposed to every wind and quite uninhabitable.

And yet this house sheltered not only the Turkish lady and Kamil, not only the Effendi with his numerous family, but also my mother and brother, and even all of our near and distant relatives who came to visit us. For as soon as the faithful Kamil got wind of any of them, he would track them down until, finding their lodgings, he removed their belongings to his mother's house, by force if need be. The kind Turkish lady was pleased by this, for, she said, the whole world's not big enough for two evil men, but a thousand good men can have a friendly chat in a walnut-shell!

Such was the house in which I spent most of each day for almost four weeks. I used to hear the old Turkish lady's voice welcoming me from her latticed windows even before I had knocked at the great front gate on Divan Yolu. My arrival would be awaited from the balcony, while my appearance would fill the house with a commotion reminiscent of a large number of birds frightened by the appearance of a cat in front of their cage. It was the voices of the women, the children, and the daughters of the Effendi, who would spring up and hasten to their harem in disorderly flight lest I should see them without their yashmaks. Kamil, with his small, snow-white turban, his long green cassock and his pale, endearing face, standing almost as tall as the forecourt wall, opened the gate to me regularly with his sweet, sad smile on his lips, bowing to the ground in a cordial salutation of welcome. The two old women always had one of my favourite sweets ready or – even more enjoyable – a fairy-tale. The Turkish lady was particularly enraptured by me because (she said), learned and wise as I was, I hadn't become an infidel idolater, but believed with all my heart in – fairy-tales! Only on two counts did she complain bitterly against me: first, that I refused to listen to any talk about the marvels of magic, and secondly that I had not yet deigned to spend a single night in her humble abode. But although it proved impossible for us to agree on the former, we finally made a compromise in respect of the latter.

From day to day we waited for her son the investigating magistrate to return. He had already sent about twenty suspects to the prisons of Constantinople, where he transferred our case in order to remain unhampered by the regional authorities. I told the old lady that when the Effendi arrived home, I would spend the night at her house. I would have much to learn. Three days later, if I am not mistaken, the examining magistrate returned. My brother, who had arrived the previous day, had much to tell me about his strenuous activities.

"I'll come tomorrow evening," I told them, "when the Effendi is here. Don't expect me any earlier."

Next day, riding one of the horses that can be hired by the Old Bridge, and not sparing the sunburned, barefoot driver who, bathed in sweat, ran all the way at the tail of the fast and obedient animal, I arrived at the house much earlier than I had promised. Thus I was not surprised when this time I did not hear the Turkish lady's welcoming voice from behind her lattice window. But when the gate opened and I saw a small boy gaping at me instead of Kamil's pale face as he made his great bow with his eternal sad smile, I had a strange and unexpected sensation. Besides the boy, no one was visible in the courtyard. Nor was there anyone in the cool, paved hall which I then entered. With some impatience I called for my mother and brother but received no reply. Unusually enough, the small door to the garden at the far end of the hall was ajar. Since I could not climb the stairs before ensuring that the harem had left the drawing-room, I went up to the door hesitantly and peeped round it into the garden.

Near the high, ivy-clad wall, sitting half in its shade, were my mother, the Turkish lady and another old woman, unveiled and in tatters, who was apparently a grimy *romio-katsivéla*, that is, a Greek-speaking Gipsy. Sitting higher than the others, she had a sieve in her lap and, leaning over it, the Turkish lady and my mother seemed to be trying, with obvious surprise and puzzlement, to comprehend something.

"It's as I say," said the Gipsy categorically after a long silence. "The murderer's near you; he's hovering about you; you needn't look far for him."

"Ha!" exclaimed my mother gleefully. "So he's been caught! He must be one of the people the Effendi sent here

in chains. I forgot to tell you the suspects are in Constantinople."

"I told you not to tell me anything without my asking,
otherwise you'll break the spell!" stormed the Pythian of
the crossroads. She gave the sieve a violent shake and the
rattle of beans was heard.

"Come now, don't get angry," said the Turkish lady. "Let's
throw them once more. Count them again."

"Hm!" said the prophetess. "Third time lucky! Very
well! But, as I said, don't tell me anything. The beans will
tell what there is to tell. Look here, mistress, I'm taking the
murderer out again." Taking a black bean out of the sieve,
she threw it over her head behind her and uttered a curse.
"Now," she went on, "you count them and I'll ask them."

My mother took the sieve, emptied the beans into her
apron and, putting it back into the Gipsy's lap, began
counting the beans one by one and replacing them with as
much care and precision as any miser counts out his precious pearls when entrusting them into another's hands.

"Are they the right number?" enquired the Gipsy, throwing her grey plaits over her shoulders.

"Yes," answered my mother. "Exactly forty."

The Gipsy picked up the sieve and, casting an expressive
glance of familiarity at the beans and shaking them twice
and thrice as though wanting to awaken the deeply slum-
bering oracular spirit within them, she called in yet more
urgent tones:

"A man's been killed and who can have killed him?
Three for the wolves and three for the thieves and three for
the soldiers on the run; three for all his secret foes, and the
beans are forty-one." As she chanted this spell she divided

the beans into groups of three, apparently allotting to each group a different attribute and a different position. "Three for the thieves and three for the wolves and three for the soldiers on the run; three for all his secret foes, and the beans are – forty-one! How many beans did you count, mistress?"

"Forty," replied my mother.

"And forty there were too," said the Gipsy. "But the murderer got among them and now there are forty-one. You see, I've put a spell on him and I'm capable of bringing him into my sieve even from the other end of the earth."

The two women having convinced themselves that the beans had miraculously increased in number, the prophetess shook the sieve repeatedly and, with the adroitness of a conjuror, tossed the contents three times in the air, each time catching them again in the sieve without dropping a single one. Then, placing the sieve on her lap and leaning over it, she gravely began to study the configurations of the beans. My mother and the Turkish lady peered in with devout attention.

"Look!" said the Gipsy after a long, reverential pause. "That's the murderer and this is you. No one is closer to you than he and your children. That's why I say, don't look for him in Constantinople, don't look for him far away. He must be a fellow-villager or a relative of yours."

The rapt curiosity with which I had been observing these events must have led me to forget that I was an eavesdropper and to lean somewhat too heavily on the garden gate. Before I knew what was happening, the door had opened with a groan and I was revealed standing behind it.

"Oh!" exclaimed mother, surprised at my unexpected

appearance. "You're here are you, my son? Why didn't Michailos come and tell me, the lazy rascal?"

Both she and the Turkish lady seemed unpleasantly surprised by the fact that their enterprise was revealed, and neither of them was able to conceal the facts from me any longer. As I have said, they knew my opposition towards superstitions and especially witches. Indeed, some days previously I had thrown a woman out for insisting on telling my fortune. They had plainly chosen that secluded corner as being the safest spot for their soothsaying, and their reproaches against my brother indicated that they had posted him at the gate to guard against my arrival, and he had betrayed his charge by allowing me to approach them unannounced. The cunning Pythian assessed the situation as soon as she saw my sullen countenance: hurriedly collecting her beans and sieve together, she made off through the other garden gate with her tail between her legs. She had doubtless had the foresight to be paid in advance. The embarrassment of the two credulous women and their incapacity to find a convenient excuse for their conduct made me regret my indiscretion. For this reason I feigned utter ignorance.

"Were you buying needles, mother?" I asked casually.

"Yes, my son!" replied my mother somewhat hesitantly. "Let's say we were buying needles so as to patch things up. When did you arrive?"

"Just this minute, mother."

"And where's that bad boy Michailos? Why didn't he come and tell me?"

"I don't know, mother. There's no one in the courtyard except the boy who opened the gate for me."

"Where can he have gone now? He can't sit still for a moment."

The Turkish lady continued to give me a cunning side-long look with a smile of disbelief on her lips and awaited my outburst of indignation at what I had seen. But instead of reproving them – which would in any case have been too late by now – I made very effort to pretend that I had seen nothing.

"Let's go inside," she said. "The Effendi will be here shortly."

Then we heard from above our heads the usual sounds of the retreating harem. Till then its denizens must have been glued to the windows overlooking the garden, observing the Gipsy's sieve-divination in reverent silence.

No sooner had we repeated the customary salutations and complimentary gestures than the entrance of the Effendi was announced. I could hardly recognize the sallow figure in European clothes that I had met before, since the sun of the countryside, while bleaching the chief surfaces of his dress, had bronzed his pale face to such an extent that one could not tell where his cheeks ended and his carefully trimmed dark beard began. The officer's oratory was as flowing on this occasion as our reception in his office had been laconic; indeed, he spoke so exquisitely as to give me qualms about the efficacy of his mission.

"Leave us to ourselves," I told the women. "The Effendi no doubt has to relate grievous details that are not suitable for your nerves."

The women went out; the Effendi looked sullen.

"I could indeed tell you frightful details," he said. "I shall not do so in order to spare you the additional grief of learning how many sins I've become responsible for! The result of my mission is at all events grievous and you must hear it. It is nil! Complete failure! Failure as regards your own case, that is, since my investigations have brought many misdemeanours to light and many culprits will get their just deserts. But our brother's murderer hasn't been found. Either he was killed in the course of the fighting that took place in the region, or it must have been the postman whom the poor man succeeded. That postman's going to drive me mad! I find him to be the proven perpetrator of many crimes, I find him the most probably suspect in our poor brother's murder, but I'm unable to find the man himself! I'm unable to arrest him! As soon as I arrived this morning I issued the strictest orders. I'm all but certain he's hiding in the capital. You know how it is: while the old woman searches for the flea in her eiderdown, it's sitting on her glasses! But don't say anything yet to the *Validé*, the *kokóna*.[5] I told Michailos the same thing. When she asked me this morning I told her my position forbids me to say anything before the court issues its verdict. Poor *kokóna*! She said nothing, but I fear she realized I had failed."

I have already said how little trust I had initially placed even in the most vigorous activities of the law in this matter, partly because of the length of time that had elapsed, partly because of the pillage and slaughter that had taken place in the district. Who knows but that the murderers had got their just deserts by perishing in the general havoc, they

---

5. *Kokóna*: Greek lady.

alone justly amid so many innocents? But when after a while I met the Effendi I altered my opinion and began to hope, as did the others, that his zeal would satisfy the law and help us to fulfil our grievous duty towards our beloved brother. The news brought by the investigating magistrate, concealing no greater failure than it confessed to, dashed those hopes irretrievably. Nothing remained for me now but to soften the effect of this intelligence on my mother by delaying as long as possible. The unfortunate Effendi, who was grieving in all honesty, agreed with me to abandon any further pursuit, especially when I assured him how my heart bled for the innocent men who had suffered hardships by being imprisoned as suspects during his strict investigations. As for the former postman, our own affair would have gained nothing by his arrest, since his alibi had repeatedly been demonstrated in court.

I thought my mother would be waiting outside the room, impatient to hear the Effendi's news. But when I stood up and looked round the door, I caught sight of her at the foot of the stairs upbraiding my brother Michailos in a low voice but none the less vehemently, whereupon, agitated as he was, he ran out of the house.

"Don't let me see you come back without Kamil!" shouted my mother after him.

"What's the matter, mother?" I enquired, seeing the misgivings that showed clearly on her face.

"Nothing, my son, nothing."

With that, she went into the kitchen without asking us about the affair, so preoccupied was she, it seemed, with Kamil's absence.

It was the first time I had seen the Effendi in his own

home. After all his labours on our behalf it was only right that I should appear as courteous and grateful to him as possible, especially since I could see how dispirited he was at the fruitlessness of those labours. So I sat next to him and we began conversing familiarly on various topics, mostly of a political nature. When in the course of our conversation I asked him what he thought of the party of the so-called Young Ottomans in Constantinople, he stood up and closed the door.

"My friend," he said, "I belong to that progressive party."

Then, taking a key from his pocket, he opened a cupboard built into the wall behind the door and continued speaking.

"My humble opinion is that the conservatives are static and that staticness is not progress."

So saying, he took a tray out of the cupboard and placed it in front of me. On the tray were a large bottle, two glasses and some saucers full of pistachios, currants and sweets.

"I mean," continued the Effendi, sitting opposite me, "that we should abandon our rusty old ideas and become animated by a new spirit and new ideas."

With that, he adroitly filled the glasses in front of us. Then I wondered whether the new spirit that animated the Young Ottomans was perhaps alcohol! I knew that many of the Effendis liked to have a secret tipple. But I could never have imagined that in a relatively short time a man could drink about an oke of neat *masticha*![6]

When they came to summon us to dinner and I saw

---

6. Oke: Ottoman unit of weight and volume, about 1¼ litres. *Masticha*: spirit flavoured with resin from the mastic tree.

that good man reeling from wall to wall, I realized why the party to which he belonged walked crabwise along the road to progress, and I felt like laughing. But when I observed the sullen look on the Turkish lady's face and my mother's perturbed expression, when I observed that some hidden misfortune made them oblivious even to the Effendi's slurred speech, some mysterious power shook my being. Clearly something that was far more grievous than the Effendi's intoxication was occurring. Time kept passing without either my brother or Kamil arriving to dine with us. The oppressive silence observed by each of us steadily increased my trepidation. My mother, however, refused to respond to my questioning glances.

"Where's Michailos, mother?" I asked her, interrupting the meal.

"He'll be here shortly, my son," she replied mournfully.

"And Kamil?" I enquired again.

My mother put her finger to her lips, signalling me in God's name to be quiet. The old Turkish lady, who hung her dejected head with indescribable grief, did not raise her eyes, but shuddered violently at the name of her son. At length she recovered.

"Don't spoil your appetite, my Sultan," she said, vainly attempting to smile. "It's nothing. Kamil went out and he's late coming back, that's all."

"Thank God!" I said, drawing breath again. "I was afraid he might be ill. Since he's well, he'll be here any moment."

"Thank God!" repeated the old lady with a deep sigh. And, as if it were intolerably hot, she opened her yashmak more than she had hitherto done in our presence and began to fan herself with the end of it. Tears welled up in the large, deep-set eyes of the old lady, whose oriental beauty now scarcely showed through her wasted features.

"Thank God he's as healthy as he is," she added.

"He's just a little pale, that's all," I said to comfort her. "Otherwise he's a healthy fellow."

"He's healthy," she sighed. "But, you see, he has this worm inside him that's eating at his heart! And if it should ever go up to his head – God preserve other people's children, and then my own! God preserve you too, my Sultan! *Karasevda* (melancholy) it's called," the old lady went on mournfully, "and it really is 'black passion'. It's broken the heart of many a mother and it's put many a brave lad under the black earth! The *kokóna* told me the story about that fellow-villager of yours who took poison at Psomathiá for Xanthoulis' daughter, and they composed a song about him and sang it in the streets. God preserve my son!"

I knew our neighbour's story. From this hint of hers I concluded what sort of passion poor Kamil was suffering from. His pale face and dreamy eyes, the signs of melancholy throughout his whole being, his intermittent fevers and his unremittingly failing health should have led me to guess the truth.

"So Kamil loves without being loved?"

"And with no hope of ever being loved," sighed his mother, "because the bitch is already married!"

"Oh," I said, "that I do not like. We must help Kamil forget her."

The unfortunate woman broke into entreaties, wishes and blessings, praises and eulogies, all of them exaggerated according to oriental custom, but all genuinely issuing from the bottom of her heart.

"If you do me this service," she said at length, "I'll become your slave; I'll sweep the threshold of your house with my eyelashes!"

"Then she began to recount the following story:

"It was before the Tobacco Monopoly was set up on Constantinople. My Kamil wasn't the sort of boy to become a *softa* and sit around doing nothing as you see him now. He had the best tobacco partnership there was. His partner used to retail the merchandise in Constantinople, while my son went round the provinces buying wholesale from the tobacco-farmers. Out there in the country he became friendly with a landowner's son. Everyone loved Kamil, he was such a sweet lad. But the landowner's son loved him too much – would that he had never been born! He loved my Kamil so much that he brought him to Constantinople and they went to the imam, who cut a vein in each one of them, and they drank each other's blood and became blood-brothers. They loved each other so much that he asked Kamil to become his brother-in-law.

"'I've got a sister on our farm, the most beautiful girl imaginable. You only have to set eyes on her and you'll lose your head.'

"Well, my Kamil was young and fine. Now the girl's father loved him, certainly, but didn't want him as a son-in-law. The father claimed to be a Sultani – that's what they call the children of the Sultan's slave-girls – and he wanted his daughter to marry a bey or a pasha. But the two lads fixed things up and the damned girl loved Kamil so much that the old man was forced to hold his tongue and swallow his indignation, he was so proud and hot-tempered. You see, he had no other daughter but Nazilé and didn't want to disappoint her. So they exchanged pledges and became engaged. The next step would have been for them to get married and come to Constantinople. But in the meantime the Monopoly had been set up, all the tobacco-shops were closed down and a lot of people were left without a job. And my Kamil not only lost a lot of money, but found himself out of work. So he went to stay at his prospective father-in-law's so as to work on the farm with the girl's brother, and he decided to live in the country for the sake of his fiancée, who didn't want to be parted from her father.

"'Kamil, my son,' I would tell him, 'a fruit that clings to the tree isn't ripe yet, and a girl who can't leave her father's house isn't ready to be a wife.'

"But Kamil loved her and did everything she asked. When the wedding-day approached, Kamil and his blood-brother got on their horses to go shopping in Constantinople. Even though the railway was nearby, the two lads loved their horses and insisted on riding into town with their gold buttons and their waistcoats, their pistols in their waist-bands and their carbines on their backs. So they set off with money in their purses and they reached the bridge at Lüleburgaz, the same bridge where your poor brother was killed later on. The bridge is high and narrow, as the Effendi told me. The river is wide and fast-flowing, with one bank bare and the other covered with wild willows and other trees that meet the wood that starts a little further off."

The drunken Effendi was in no position to vouch for the accuracy of the description, for he had already been lying snoring near the table for some time.

"As soon as they had reached the middle of the bridge," the old lady went on, "Kamil saw a flash through the willows and heard a shot. And before he knew where he was, he saw his comrade fall wounded. Kamil's horse shied and turned aside and broke through the railings of the bridge, falling into the river with my son on its back. God preserve people from such an accident! Who knows how long he wrestled with death? But, you see, he was fated to live. The horse was found dead, but he escaped! For three days he didn't know where he was. When he came to a little, he realized he was at a mill – the current had carried him along tangled in the horse's reins. If the miller hadn't managed to save him at the last moment... So be it! The miller wasn't such a good man because when my son came to he realized he'd taken his money-belt. He didn't say anything, though, because he would willingly have handed it over to him in any case. So he thanked him as best he could and set off for his father-in-law's farm to see whether his blood-brother had come to harm and to bring the news. But when he reached the door, more dead than alive, the old man wouldn't let him in. He turned his face away so as not to see him.

"'You let your blood-brother be killed,' he told him, 'without firing a shot, and now you come to my house without the murderer's head in your hands! You're a coward and a deceiver!'

"And he kicked him out and shut the door! With no life in his body and no money in his pocket! Who knows on what plain his bones would now lie scattered had he not had the good fortune to stumble on your village and had this saintly woman, the *Validé* your mother, not taken him into her house and looked after him? We Turks say that all Christians will go to Hell; but when I think of the good deed your mother did, I say to myself, 'If that Christian doesn't go to Paradise, then I don't know what Turk will go!' But no one knows God's will!

"All that time I had given up my son for lost. We'd heard about his blood-brother's murder, but the Effendi wasn't in the police yet, and the Sultani, Kamil's so-called father-in-law, claimed he hadn't seen him. So we reckoned he was dead. When your brother came and brought him all skin and bones and deathly pale, he looked as if he'd risen from the grave. God grant that you have such joy in your life, my son, as I felt that day! It took a long time, it's true, but in the end my son got better. But as soon as he was well again, he got up to leave.

"'Where are you going, my son?'

"'To my fiancée, mother, and my father-in-law.'

"'What do you want with such a father-in-law, my son? Let him go hang!"

"'No, mother, there's no other way. He must find out that I'm neither a coward nor a deceiver. I must talk to him.'

"So off he went. After a couple of weeks he came back unexpectedly; but he was a changed man! He made no mention of where he'd been and what he'd one. But no sooner had he arrived than he took to his bed with a fever. It was January.

"'Didn't I tell you not to go travelling in the middle of winter, my son? There, you've made yourself ill again!'

"'Better to have died from the winter's cold than to have suffered what I've suffered, mother!'

"That was all he said to me, but he gave me the pledges we had sent the Sultani's daughter when he became engaged to her. Then I understood why he was ill: the bitch had married someone else! May God punish her! She's responsible for my son getting into this state. You can see what's happened to him! Out of his grief he's registered as a novice at the local dervishes' monastery and he goes every Friday and takes opium with the dervishes, and kneels with them and groans till his innards are all wrenched about, and he beats his chest until they carry him out in a faint. As if that wasn't enough, the Sheikh, the leader of the dervishes, has taken a great liking to him and has told me that one day my son will become a saint. But there's one thing that happens to him sometimes that'll make me lose my mind! You've seen how calm and mild and quiet he is. He became like that when he found out his fiancée had got married, much more so than he was before. But occasionally you see him getting wild and agitated, and he doesn't know what he's doing – it's as if he's trying to burst out of his clothes! Today, for instance, while we were out in the garden with the Gipsy, he charged into the house like a madman, snatched something out of the cupboard and rushed out again. We didn't see him, but Michailos, who we'd got to wait at the door for you, saw him and put his arms out to stop him. But it was as if he saw the devil himself in front of him – he let out a curse and knocked Michailos to the ground as he rushed out. That's why my son didn't answer the door to you today, and that's why you found no one to welcome you. Because, when he came to, Michailos ran after Kamil to see if he could catch him, but he wasn't able to. He came back to tell us what happened, then went out again to see if he could find him somewhere near the sea… God preserve my son from the sea!"

The old lady sighed and let her floods of tears flow.

Dinner that evening ended quite differently than I had

imagined it. Here, snoring and brutishly drunk, was that zealous and energetic investigating magistrate, whom hitherto I had thought to be the model of a sober and devoted public servant. There, lamenting and plunged into utter misery, was the old lady who for so many days had been preparing to celebrate the evening of my sojourn at her house with all manner of Turkish entertainments, and who this evening found no solace even in my mother's tender care. And Kamil – prudent, restrained Kamil, who drank holy water and kissed the priest's hand, and chiefly for whose sake I had forgotten my dislike of his co-religionists – was suddenly presented to me as belonging to the most fanatical order of groaning dervishes and as a man of ill fortune whose mind, whether through an unhappy love-affair or an excessive use of opium, was deranged and subject to periodic fits of dementia. And yet for a moment I thought of going out myself in search of him. But apart from the fact that I would not know where to go, I called to mind his meek and pious nature and imagined how adversely his sickly disposition might be affected by the idea that his misery was being witnessed by me, whom he so especially honoured and respected. Since time was passing and neither my brother nor Kamil had returned, I addressed the women.

"I have an idea. Michailos must surely have found Kamil, but after what has happened Kamil, bashful as he is, will refuse to come home because he knows I am here."

"You've got it!" said my mother. "Perhaps they're walking about in the street, waiting for the living-room light to go out so they can come in. Come, my son, let's not worry the *hanum* any more; I'll show you where you're sleeping."

After some ineffectual words of comfort to the long-suffering Turkish lady, my mother walked ahead of me holding a small oil-lamp.

"We've made your bed in the kiosk," she told me as we descended the stairs. "You're a light sleeper and the children wake up early and make a lot of noise. So we've made your bed there."

When my mother opened the pavilion door, my nostrils were assailed by the scent of some burning aromatic wood. Everything in the house looked exceptionally tidy, but I was so dispirited when I entered that I was unable to scrutinize the contents. My heart was in thrall to a vague anxiety, the lurking presentiment of some unknown misfortune. Thus, when my mother began asking me about the Effendi's report on my brother's murderer, I was, I remember, exceedingly enigmatic and laconic, unconsciously pitying her.

For some time after my mother left, I sat cross-legged on the red rug covering the low sofa, leaning towards the dim light of a wretched lamp and trying to dispel my thoughts and the vivid images of my fancy by reading I know not what book. But the objects of my mental vision, which were far brighter than the pages, interposed themselves between me and the book, and all the time my reading was but a mechanical promenade of my eyes over the lines of each page. Twice or thrice I lay down on my fragrant bed, vainly forcing my eyes to remain closed. The scent of the musk emanating from the hand-embroidered pillows, intoxicating and stupefying as it was, had no power to lull my heightened emotions. The story of the unfortunate Kamil kept unfolding before my closed eyes in vivid

pictures. How affable, how talkative must he once have
been, this solitary, taciturn and hence tiresome *softa*, who
had so unusually won the friendship of one of the Sultanis
who, despite their progressive impoverishment, hold the
most self-important position in the Ottoman aristocracy!
And what a friendship it must have been! What a blood-
brotherhood! The young Sultani doubtless derived a greater
than usual felicity from it, and out of fraternal love hastened
to let his beautiful sister share it. Now I imagined Kamil,
secretly and idyllically in love with his prospective fiancée,
partaking in thrills and emotions usually unknown to his
co-religionists but yet suited to his sensitive heart. Then I
imagined him taming a headstrong horse and galloping beside his blood-brother in the striking, vividly-coloured costume of young men in the provinces, his weapons gleam-
ing; and then again I imagined him in fearful confusion,
hurtling down from the high bridge with his runaway horse
and desperately wrestling with the animal's frenzy, with the
fury of the violent currents, with death itself, as my mother
had put it, until finally, exhausted, he let himself be swept
along, probably entangled in the stirrup-straps, both he and
his already expiring horse the playthings of the rushing waters. Then that sullen, selfish, inhuman Sultani mercilessly
closing the door on his daughter's half-dead fiancé! Then
again poor Kamil pitilessly cast up near old Mourtos' inn,
doomed in his penury to be racked by fever and yet exposed to the night frost and the midday heat, pleading de-
mentedly for mercy from a bush (perhaps his fiancée) and
threatening to slaughter a wild artichoke (perhaps his
blood-brother's murderer)! How could the unfortunate
young man find the murderer? How was he to avenge his

blood-brother? Why did the girl abandon him when she should have loved him all the more? Kamil's mild character must have prevented him from taking the law into his own hands and carrying out his stern and bloody duty, and rather than commit a crime in order to satisfy his father-in-law's ferocious heart, he must have preferred to kill his own heart by destroying its happiness. Perhaps he would have done better not to have made an exception, but to have acted like a true Ottoman, avenging his blood-brother according to that barbaric custom that the law of his fellows overlooks, and which even the most benevolent of religions has not succeeded in eradicating among Christians.

Such were the images and thoughts that were occupying when the sound of footsteps at the entrance to the pavilion made me spring up suddenly from where I lay. On entering I had seen some bedding on the floor. Perhaps it was my brother, I thought to myself, and I opened the door. In the semi-darkness inside the entrance I made out the faint outline of Kamil, lean and tall, his phosphorescent white turban almost touching the ceiling.

"Do they know you've come, Kamil? Your mother was very anxious," I said, trying to hide my own anxiety.

"It's all over now!" said Kamil, rooted to the spot, his voice inexplicably unfamiliar. "The deed is done. She'll get some peace and so will I."

"Good, Kamil!" I said, encouraging him to follow me into my room. "I know you're a sensible chap. I know this will be the last time."

"Yes," said Kamil confidently. "The last!"

But what was my surprise when I saw him coming into the room! His pale visage, in which were reflected the white of his turban and the green of his cassock, resembled the face of one long dead. His lips were livid, his eyes expressionless, and his movements were like those of a corpse under the influence of some mysterious galvanism. The incessant flickering of my dim lamp agitatedly reflecting against him rendered his appearance eerily frightful, like the apparition of a deathly spectre. I do not know how I managed to preserve my composure, but I still remember with horror that I embraced and kissed him to give him courage, so great was my pity for the poor wretch! When he had calmed down somewhat, he took a deep breath and spoke.

"Now it's all over! Now I'll get some peace!"

And he uttered an obscene curse against a third person, calling him by an insulting name.

"He wasn't content to kill my blood-brother," he went on. "He wasn't content to ruin my health and happiness. He used to come every so often and poison the wretched life that was left in me!"

When he saw that I could find nothing to say to him, he continued:

"I know. You're a learned man and you'll laugh. That's why I didn't tell you anything before now. But the Sheikh of our monastery is more learned than you; he's a saint, and whoever does his bidding carries out God's will. The vampire's been haunting me for three years now, and no one could save me. Whenever I went to a festival he was there; whenever I went to market he was there; until he drove me to despair and I gave up my job and became a *softa*. A good thing I did, because our Sheikh saved me! May we have his blessing! 'Don't get taken in because he looks like a dead man,' he told me. 'A vampire is just a skin full of blood. Bring me a black-handled knife and I'll bless it for you. Then when you next see him, pierce him so the blood runs out, and he'll never cross your path again.'"

Then I noticed to my horror that his hands were covered in blood and his clothes were stained. A cold sweat came over me.

"Oh, Kamil, you've shed blood!"

"No! It's just the vampire's blood, the dead man's blood."

"Which dead man's ghost was it?" I asked, my limbs trembling.

"The man that killed my blood-brother," he replied.

"And who killed your blood-brother's murderer?"

"Who else had that duty but I?" responded the Turk with a pride that disgusted me.

"How can it be? What a calamity!" I stammered almost involuntarily.

"Ha!" exclaimed the Turk. "Isn't it written in your book, 'They that live by the sword shall perish by the sword'? Whenever the devil makes a bullet for a murderer, he makes another for the avenger. So listen here. Maybe you don't know that my blood-brother's murderer put me at death's door and caused me to be robbed by a miller, to be thrown out by my father-in-law, and to fetch up in a terrible state at your village. Well, now you know. When I came back to Constantinople from your house and felt fit again, I took my gun and went back to the miller who got me out of the river half-dead.

"'You stole my purse,' I told him, 'with 500 florins in it. You saved my life, but that's not worth ten *paras*. Since you're always nosing about by the riverside, you must know who killed my blood-brother the day you fished me out. See, my gun's cocked! If you tell me I'll let you keep what you took, but if you keep your secret you'll lose your life!' That's what I told him, and I was right because the miller was a cowardly crook, and when he saw he was in a fix he said:

"'Promise you won't do the killing in my mill and I'll show you your man.'

"I promised.

"'Hide behind here,' he said. 'Any moment now someone'll come in with a mail-bag and a gun over his shoulder. He's the one who killed the Sultani's son. He's called Charalambis, Mitakos' son. Every fortnight he crosses the bridge where you fell with your horse.'"

My ears were ringing so loudly that I could scarcely hear him. The Turk continued:

"But before I had time to hide, there was the villain coming in just as the miller had told me. I kept my gun cocked, but I'd given my word. I was afraid he might realize what was going on and I'd be forced to break my promise. So I went out and set off towards the bridge. But it was winter and there were no leaves on the trees, and since he was on his guard he got wind of me before he climbed to the middle of the bridge, so he turned back and began running. I went after him as fast as I could, but he was too quick for me. I fired at him twice and each time the villain fired back on the run. 'All right,' I said to myself. 'Wherever you go, you've got to cross the bridge again!'"

So that was the blood my poor brother had told my mother about, which haunted the murderer on the road and forced him to turn back and resign his job in the post!

My hair stood on end, my limbs trembled like autumn leaves, and I could no longer master my senses.

The Turk went on:

"A fortnight went by and I lay in wait for him all the time. Fighting had broken out. The local governor had closed the Lüleburgaz railway and ordered everyone to flee to Constantinople; but I didn't budge. If one more night had passed, the Russians would have killed me. But God preserved me and sent me my man."

Cold sweat poured from my brow. I remember that I twice made to lunge at him and stifle his confession in his throat, but I was transfixed by terror. While I imagined I was moving, in reality I remained inert as if I had become paralysed.

The Turk went on:

"This time I was well hidden and, so that he wouldn't suspect anything, I let him cross the bridge. When I saw him go down to the river and bend down to drink I waited a moment so as not to commit a sin. Then I fired..."

"Oh wretched man! You murdered my brother!"

At that moment I heard from the garden a confused noise in which I recognized my young brother's voice shouting:

"Here! He's sleeping in here!"

Torch-flames cast blood-red glimmers on the ivy-clad walls, and a flash of swords and guns burst through the little gate towards the pavilion. It was the police! My door flew open with a clatter and my brother entered first.

"Let them take him away!" he shouted. "He's a murderer! He killed Charalambis! He killed him before my very eyes!"

The room filled with watchmen, firemen and police-

men. Kamil, rooted to the spot, let himself be bound with
no show or resistance or emotion. The officer in charge
stepped forward from the crowd and politely saluted me.

"Sir, what coincidence," he said, "what strange coincidence brings you to the murderer's house?"

I scarcely recognized him. I had come into contact with
him during my frequent visits to the police ministry; he
knew the details of our case and his every effort to expedite
it had been rewarded. I took him aside and explained to
him that Kamil, who was gazing at us coolly and dispas-
sionately, had killed my brother, believing that he was
avenging the murder of his blood-brother, and had that
night killed the guilty postman who was sought by the police and whose real presence he took for a demonic apparition come to haunt him. The officer shook my hand ami-
cably and led his captive away.

Early the following morning my mother left that
hideous house at my persistent request and returned di-
rectly to our village. It was in no way expedient that she
should learn the truth.

About three years had passed since that night, when I found
myself entering our village for the first time since I had left
it while still a child. The many misfortunes supervening in
the meantime had somehow overshadowed those old times;
but the closer I came to our house, the more clearly did its
sad story emerge from the depths of the years and the more
did the past become renewed. My carriage was already
passing by a dilapidated and deserted house. Anyone else
would have felt a deeply elegiac sorrow if, on returning

from a long absence, he found the silence of death where he had left the vibrancy and gaiety of life, destruction and desolation where he had left comfort and well-being. But the closed windows, the cracked walls, the overgrown yard, the unfenced garden exposed to every bane produced an incongruous sense of satisfaction in me. It seemed to me that I would have been saddened had that house continued to flourish. For it was the house of Mitakos, the house of Lambis, the former postman, whom I could not but hold responsible for the murder of my unfortunate brother. The actual murderer had lost his reason in front of me during the first judicial hearing as soon as he ascertained whose heart had been pierced by the bullet that he had intended for his blood-brother's murderer. As the target of that shot, fired in blind revenge, the wicked son of Mitakos had with unholy cunning substituted the breast of my poor brother, who had the misfortune to resemble him not only in height and attitude but also in dress. It was now proven that for this purpose alone he had inveigled the trusting young man into taking over his duties, and it was established that he was so certain as to the consequences of his abominable wickedness that he had maliciously predicted the very hour at which my brother was to meet his end.

When I arrived outside our house, I was surprised to see a filthy, ragged, barefoot dervish come out of the yard and run to open the carriage door.

"*Aman, Sultanim! Kokona bilmesin!*"

I gave a violent shudder of horror. Those were the demented words that Kamil had uttered in the court-room before swooning at my feet!

"For mercy's sake, my Sultan! Don't let the lady find out!"

The frightful sound of his voice, which seemed to emanate from a deep tomb rather than from a human mouth, so disturbed me that when I threw myself into the arms of my mother, who hastened to welcome me, I know not what strange mixture of disgust and pity filled my heart.

Thus I entered the yard, turning my back on the abomination that was following me. The garden gate was open on the far side of our house. In this garden there still flourishes an apple-tree, under whose shade my brothers and I used to play so happily. But those resonant voices and our childish laughter are no longer to be heard there. Eternal silence reigns and a white stone cross, before which there burns a sleepless icon-lamp, bears witness to the sanctity of the place: for it is there that my much-lamented brother lies buried. Thither I tearfully directed my steps. His resting-place was adorned with the most splendid, the most exquisite roses. Our garden had once been neglected. Now it was full of flowers that seemed as if they had shot forth from that tomb and had gradually spread into the further corners of the garden.

"Poor Kamil's growing them!" whispered my mother mournfully.

I gave a renewed shudder. Turning with convulsively trembling lips towards the creature about whom she spoke, I told him:

"I command you never to set foot in our house again!"

"Oh, the poor dear!" exclaimed my mother with indescribable anguish. "You're wasting your breath, my son. The poor wretch can neither hear nor speak any more! He's mad!"

Kamil fixed his lustreless eyes on the horizon like a

man completely unaware of what was happening about him. On his head he now wore a dervish's conical hat with a green sash round it, which made him look ridiculously tall. The kaftan of the monastic order to which he belonged now hung in tatters about his emaciated body. His elbows protruded through the rents in his garments, but around his waist he wore a splendid leather belt with a buckle bearing a large onyx from Mecca. His face, however, either because of the state of impassivity in which he now lived, or through the influence of the sun, had a healthier appearance than before.

"Let them go hang!" said my mother, looking at him with pity in her eyes. "They've made him a saint! After he went mad they made him a saint! They kiss his hand and bring him food and clothes, and they want to take him to the governor's house. But he only eats dry bread, he only wears what you see there, and he sleeps on the floor of the barn. He refuses to leave me whatever they do. Only, when they upset him too much or he gets agitated, he lets out a strange cry: 'For mercy's sake, my Sultan! Don't let the lady find out!' That's all he's capable of saying! Poor Kamil!"

As she spoke I recalled her once implacable fury against the murderer, her complaints that our poor brother was disturbed in his grave whenever his murderer trod the earth, albeit at the other end of the world. I shuddered at the thought that the murderer was daily walking over the grave of his victim, and I trembled lest the unfortunate woman should find out. That might have killed her.

"Nevertheless," I told her, "if you send him away I'm sure he'll go back to his own people. Do me the favour of sending him away."

"What do you mean?" she exclaimed, almost in tears. "I sometimes remember that wagtail who kicked him out of our room, and I wish I had an arm that stretched from here to Constantinople so I could slap his womanly face, and here you are telling me to throw him out with my own hands! He's left his own mother to come to me. He fetches water, goes to the mill, takes the bread to the bakery, hoes the vines, sweeps the yard, grows the flowers on Christakis' grave – he even insists on lighting the icon-lamp himself. How can I throw him out after I looked after him for seven months in bed like my own child? May God punish who-ever brought him to such a terrible state! Please, I beg you, my son, leave the poor lad to his calamities and tell me, have they found the murderer? I don't suppose they have!"

"No," I replied, as I saw him before me.

For I pondered what she had told me about him: I com-pared the simple-minded innocence of the lunatic with the abominable wickedness of the former postman, and I could not tell which was my brother's murderer.